The Hong Kong Economic Policy Studies Series

TOURISM AND
THE HONG KONG ECONOMY

TOURISM AND
THE HONG KONG ECONOMY

Kai-Sun Kwong

Published for
The Hong Kong Centre for Economic Research
The Better Hong Kong Foundation
The Hong Kong Economic Policy Studies Forum
by

City University of Hong Kong Press

First published 1997
Printed in Hong Kong

ISBN 962-937-009-3

Published by
City University of Hong Kong Press
City University of Hong Kong
Tat Chee Avenue, Kowloon, Hong Kong

Internet: http://www.cityu.edu.hk/upress/
E-mail: upress@cityu.edu.hk

The free-style calligraphy on the cover, *lü*, means "tour" in Chinese.

Contents

Detailed Chapter Contents

Foreword

The key to the economic success of Hong Kong has been a business and policy environment which is simple, predictable and transparent. Experience shows that prosperity results from policies that protect private property rights, maintain open and competitive markets, and limit the role of the government.

The rapid structural change of Hong Kong's economy in recent years has generated considerable debate over the proper role of economic policy in the future. The restoration of sovereignty over Hong Kong from Britain to China has further complicated the debate. Anxiety persists as to whether the pre-1997 business and policy environment of Hong Kong will continue.

During this period of economic and political transition in Hong Kong, various interested parties will be re-assessing Hong Kong's existing economic policies. Inevitably, some will advocate an agenda aimed at altering the present policy making framework to reshape the future course of public policy.

For this reason, it is of paramount importance for those familiar with economic affairs to reiterate the reasons behind the success of the economic system in the past, to identify what the challenges are for the future, to analyze and understand the economy sector by sector, and to develop appropriate policy solutions to achieve continued prosperity.

In a conversation with my colleague Y. F. Luk, we came upon the idea of inviting economists from universities in Hong Kong to take up the challenge of examining systematically the economic policy issues of Hong Kong. An expanding group of economists (The Hong Kong Economic Policy Studies Forum) met several times to give form and shape to our initial ideas. The Hong Kong Economic Policy Studies Project was then launched in 1996 with some 30 economists from the universities in Hong Kong and a few from overseas. This is the first time in Hong Kong history that a concerted public effort has been undertaken by academic economists in the territory. It represents a joint expression of our collective concerns, our hopes for a better Hong Kong, and our faith in the economic future.

The Hong Kong Centre for Economic Research is privileged to be co-ordinating this Project. We are particularly grateful to The Better Hong Kong Foundation whose support and assistance has made it possible for us to conduct the present study, the results of which are published in this monograph. We also thank the directors and editors of the City University of Hong Kong Press and The Commercial Press (H.K.) Ltd. for their enthusiasm and dedication which extends far beyond the call of duty. The unfailing support of many distinguished citizens in our endeavour and their words of encouragement are especially gratifying.

> Yue-Chim Richard Wong
> Director
> The Hong Kong Centre
> for Economic Research

Foreword by the Series Editor

Generally speaking, suppliers of most services have to sell their output to consumers directly and at the spot. As a result, unlike manufactured products which can be sold worldwide, services are relatively restricted in terms of the coverage of business and the volume of sales .

Yet, it is not necessarily true that all services sales are confined geographically, and exports do not have to be interpreted as only manufactured products leaving the domestic economy. As a type of service, tourism too, can be exported.

Hong Kong serves in various ways tourists arriving from all continents, and thus "exports" tourist services to the rest of the world. As a matter of fact, tourist services account for the largest proportion of all services exports of Hong Kong. Given the shift to a services economy and the significant role of tourism in services, the tourist industry deserves close attention and warrants detailed analysis and understanding.

From the point of view of value-added, tourism is not a distinct and monolithic industry. Instead, it is composed of various parts of different economic sectors including transportation, hotel, retailing, sight-seeing, entertainment, telecommunications, and restaurants. To understand tourism in Hong Kong in detail, it is necessary to go into these parts separately.

What is the current state of tourism in Hong Kong? What are the interactions between tourism and the economy? How have the sources, flows, and expenditure patterns of tourists changed in recent years? Do Hong Kong's facilities in transport, hotel, dining and retail match well? What policies can the government take to further enhance tourism in Hong Kong?

Based on detailed data analysis, this book addresses the above questions and discusses the future of Hong Kong tourism. The author, Dr. Kai-sun Kwong, looks at tourism from the broad perspective of the economy. He also puts Hong Kong in the wider contexts of Southern China and the Asia-Pacific region. He further makes policy proposals regarding air services, hotel, tourist sites, and others.

Given Hong Kong's historical background, geographical location, economic strength and future promise, there is certainly great potential for tourism which will continue to be an important part of the economy. This book provides good reference materials to those who are concerned with the economy of Hong Kong in general and tourism in particular.

Y. F. Luk
School of Economics and Finance
The University of Hong Kong

Preface

In the course of research, I have benefited from the input of a large number of professionals in the tourism sector. Chief among them are: Tina Cheng, Ricky Cheung, Mabel Hung, Elsie Lo, Kenneth Hayden Sadler, and Stanley Yip at the Hong Kong Tourist Association (HKTA); James Lu at the Hong Kong Hotels Association, and Dennis Sun of The Better Hong Kong Foundation. They have given me valuable insight into the many aspects of the sector. Ricky Cheung, in particular, has been most helpful in providing me with the data collected by the HKTA and the study reports in their archives. I should therefore express my hearty thanks to all of them.

I should also thank the Hong Kong Centre for Economic Research for initiating this study, for their comments on an earlier draft, and for their valuable editorial assistance. Two anonymous referees have graciously read through an earlier draft. For their comments, which span dozens of pages, I wish I could have the chance to thank them in person. The City University of Hong Kong Press has done an admirable job in getting the book out in print in record time.

My thanks also go to The Better Hong Kong Foundation for supporting and lending weight to this study. It is often said that, "A book is seldom worth the efforts that have gone into writing it." To me, however, with all the help that I have got, writing the present monograph has been a most enjoyable experience.

Kai-Sun Kwong
Department of Economics
The Chinese University of Hong Kong

List of Illustrations

Figure

Tables

xvii

CHAPTER 1

Tourism: The Cornerstone of the Export of Services

Introduction

More than 10 million visitors came to Hong Kong in 1995, almost twice its total population, spending almost HK$73 billion. As a sector that exports services, tourism occupies a dominant position in the economy. Tourism accounted for a share of some 40% of all services exports in 1995, putting it far ahead of other sectors of the service industry. Yet the Hong Kong government has no specific policy to promote tourism, and there is no department within the civil service charged with the responsibility of regulating and developing tourism. Instead, the task of promoting tourism activities in Hong Kong rests solely with the Hong Kong Tourist Association (HKTA) which is a government-funded organization outside the formal structure of the civil service.

Is this an indication that the government does not understand the importance of the tourism sector? What are the policy blind spots? Are there structural bottlenecks?

Before these questions can be answered, it would be beneficial for this introductory chapter to provide the background information needed for the economic analysis made in this book. Covered here are such topics as the nature of Hong Kong as a tourist city, its relations with China, types of "tourists", and problems of volatility in tourism business. After these preliminaries, the chapter discusses the components of tourism, especially the "business hub" trend and the China factor. The economic importance of tourism is then

1

addressed to, followed by a summary of the themes in Chapter 2 through Chapter 8 where specific issues are discussed.

Hong Kong is a metropolitan city, a centre where people from all over the world meet, confer, negotiate, consult, seek information, and strike deals. It is not a vacation resort destination along the business lines of Indonesia's Bali or the Maldives in the Indian Ocean. Visitors do not come to Hong Kong just for relaxing beach holidays. Hong Kong has the advantages and attractions of a big city as well. A significant proportion of visitors to Hong Kong are business travellers, not tourists, although tourism statistics do not necessarily make a distinction between the two types of visitors. To the business public, Hong Kong offers a wide range of business services — legal, accounting, consulting, financial, and trading — functions to which other major cities of the world also owe their continued prosperity. Of course, Hong Kong has managed to attract visitors who come purely for pleasure. In Hong Kong, visitors can eat well, sample a large variety of consumer goods, spot the latest fashion trends, see technology in action, and generally witness the way a fast-paced society operates. Some visitors find Hong Kong an exciting place to explore, for there is nothing barring them from experiencing first hand the idiosyncrasies of this unusual city. In Hong Kong, visitors and residents frequently mingle. They share the same facilities. So-called tourist attractions, which are no longer restricted to the hotel districts and a few landmarks, are actually very much a part of the lives of local residents.

For the purpose of the present study, the term *tourists* takes on a larger meaning than is normally understood by the word. Tourists in the present study include all visitors who enter Hong Kong — in other words, all travellers who are not Hong Kong residents and who enter Hong Kong for reasons other than simply to continue to another destination. Transit passengers are excluded from discussion because they add relatively little to the economy of Hong Kong. Included in the discussion are tourists from Japan, the People's Republic of China, Taiwan, the United States and so on who come to Hong Kong as a final destination for the purpose of shopping and sightseeing; visitors who stay for a day or two (somewhat longer for visitors from the People's Republic of China) *en route* to or from another destination; and business travellers from around the world.

There is a large body of knowledge concerning tourism promotion — ways to create new marketing concepts, orchestrate new events, organize overseas marketing offices, connect with overseas travel agencies and wholesalers, co-ordinate with airlines and hotels, explore new sources of visitors, disseminate information to visitors before and after they arrive, and monitor the standard of local service providers such as restaurants, retailers, tour guides and so on — in short, the professional aspects of tourism. In Hong Kong, these promotional tasks are largely undertaken by the Hong Kong Tourist Association.

The present study offers a less professional perspective on tourism, albeit one that is wider and more in keeping with the significance of tourism for Hong Kong's economic development. The income that tourism brings to the economy is the underlying motivation of the study, especially in the context of the changing nature of the Hong Kong economy in regard to service. Tourism embodies a number of supporting sectors. Chief among these are airlines, airports, retail shops, hotels, and tourist attractions. The strengths and weaknesses of these sectors, together with the constraints that they may impose on tourism development, constitute the focus of the present study.

Hong Kong is a city of China. It is China's door to the world. In terms of tourism, the identity of Hong Kong takes on special meaning. Every country in the world has a number of gateway cities — New York and Los Angeles in the United States, Tokyo and Osaka in Japan, and London in the United Kingdom, to give a few examples. These gateway cities are channels that connect different parts of the countries to the outside world, and vice versa. Hong Kong performs such a function for China. The major difference is that Hong Kong is separate from the rest of China in fiscal terms. In comparison with other gateway cities, Hong Kong has more autonomy. Income earned from tourism accrues directly and exclusively to the people of Hong Kong, not to those of China at large. Tourism has the potential to become a significant engine of Hong Kong's economic growth.

Tourism in Hong Kong as a gateway city is set for rapid growth. There are 1,200 million people in China, 200 times that of Hong Kong. Many of these people are amassing wealth quickly, and most have never travelled outside China. Until now, the flow of tourists out of China has been restrained by institutional measures. As these restraints are gradually lifted, the volume of tourists coming *to* Hong Kong from China and passing *through* Hong Kong on their way from China to destinations elsewhere in the world will be pathbreaking.

China itself has an enormous potential to attract many more tourists. Its landscape, natural habitats, archaeological discoveries, historical heritage, and large variety of cultures are still largely unknown to the world. Few countries can offer travel experiences as new and exciting as China can. In addition, there are still strong cultural ties between tens of million overseas Chinese and those who live in China. As China develops and becomes more tourism oriented, the number of overseas Chinese travelling to China will be huge. In general, tourism in China is on the verge of rapid expansion, as is the volume of Chinese people living in China who will be travelling outside the country. Hong Kong is going to benefit from this trend. Hong Kong does not want to be just a gateway that serves China. Instead, Hong Kong ought to add value to the trips of the China-originated and China-bound traffic. In the process, income will be created for the people of Hong Kong, and economic growth will be stimulated.

A number of bottlenecks that restrain tourism growth can easily arise. The crux of the matter is that many investors in the tourism business perceive their business environment as being rather volatile and unpredictable. Despite the long-term growth trend, transitory setbacks have been common. Commonly cited unforeseen events include the oil crises of 1976 and 1981, which led to a worldwide recession; the incident of 4 June 1989 in Beijing, which deterred western tourists from visiting China; the Gulf War of 1990–91, which reduced tourist outflow from the West, particularly from the United States; and the Thousand Island Lake incident[1] of 1995, which deterred Taiwanese tourists from visiting China. Investors learn from these lessons and are generally cautious about expanding capacity. The delays in expansion have caused the emergence of systemic capacity constraints.

The volatility of the tourism business is attributable to a number of sources. Besides the political events and accidents mentioned above, the tourism business has been perceived to be both income and price sensitive. The demand for travel depends, to a great degree, on consumer income which in turn depends on global economic conditions. As for price sensitivity, changes in exchange rates, local hotel costs, airfare, and costs in other tourist destinations could affect the tourism business in Hong Kong. It must be pointed out, however, that about 30% of visitors to Hong Kong are business travellers. To the extent that business travelling is less sensitive to income and prices than vacation travelling, Hong Kong's tourism sector is perhaps less volatile than those of most other destinations in the region.

Components of Tourism

Unlike the manufacturing sector or the financial sector, tourism is not a separate sector in formal systems of classification. Tourism is rather a combination of sectors. In the case of Hong Kong, tourism consists of air, sea, and land transportation; hotels and restaurants; public transport; and retail outlets. These are, of course, services that cater to locals as much as to visitors. So it is not easy to measure the contribution of tourism to the local economy.

The fact that visitors and locals mingle means that enhancing tourism facilities usually has a favourable impact on the quality of life of Hong Kong. For example, the building of new hotels provides a high-quality environment for business activities such as conferences and for leisure activities such as shopping and dining.

A large component of tourism is transportation. Most visitors come to Hong Kong by air. If they fly with a local airline, then Hong Kong is exporting a service, and part of the airfare contributes to the income of Hong Kong. The same holds true for land and sea transportation. In recent years, the number of visitors from China has risen rapidly, and land transport has become increasingly important as a mode of visitor transportation.

Hotels are another major component of tourism. Hotels derive their business from two principal sources — room rentals and food sales. Whereas locals are responsible for a significant portion of food sales, room rentals are accounted for almost entirely by visitors. Room rentals hold, by far, the largest share of hotel receipts, accounting for about half of them. The balance of the receipts is accounted for principally by food and beverage sales, with other items such as retail shop rentals and long-distance telephone and laundry charges playing relatively minor roles.

The retail sector is also an important component of tourism. Hong Kong is perhaps unique in this regard. While visitors come to Hong Kong for many reasons, they consistently spend as much on shopping as they do on hotel bills, meals eaten outside hotels, and tours combined. Of course, the amount visitors spend on retail items is still small relative to what locals spend. Nevertheless, in the cases of fashion clothing, leather goods, jewellery, and cosmetics, visitors' expenditures make up a significant share of total purchases.

There are also other less important but not inconsequential tourism-related businesses. Taxis, ferries, night clubs, bars, and tourist attractions such as Ocean Park, The Peak, and Repulse Bay all derive significant revenue from tourists.

Robustness of Business Hub

There are indications that Hong Kong is following in the footsteps of world-class cities such as New York, London, and Tokyo. These cities are centres of trade, finance, transport, culture, entertainment, and business services. That they can perform such diverse functions is interesting. What the world's big cities have in common is that they were all originally important seaports. Most started as ports with good access to waterways, establishing themselves as trading posts. Buyers and sellers from the surrounding region congregated in the cities, and large volumes of goods changed hands. Later, factories were set up to supply manufactured goods to the market. As market activities flourished, people became richer, and wage rates increased. Gradually, manufacturing activities shifted to cheaper places. Cities became nerve centres that collected and processed information and co-ordinated activities taking place in different locations. The residents of cities were better educated and more sophisticated than those of rural areas. Their higher incomes and effective social networking supported the emergence of financial activities. Banks and commodity and stock exchanges were set up in cities, with businesses extending far beyond city boundaries. As cities handled a large flow of travellers and goods, transport infrastructure within cities, and, more importantly, that which connected the cities with other parts of the world, became crucially important. As a result, railway networks evolved around cities. After the Second World War, as civil aviation loomed large, airports were built in cities, and air routes evolved around cities as well. In addition, the high concentration of educated, high-income people in cities fostered flourishing artistic communities and sports and entertainment activities. Museums, theatres, concert halls, and stadiums were built. Cities became not only centres of business but also centres of culture.

The important lesson that can be drawn from the experience of big cities is that activities that take place in cities tend to feed on themselves. As banks start up offices in a city, more banks will be attracted to do the same. As more companies are listed on the stock exchange, more companies will go for a listing. As more retailers set up outlets, more shoppers will gather to compare merchandises and prices, and they in turn will attract more retailers. And the same positive feedback idea goes for insurance companies, legal and accounting firms, and airline, shipping and telecommunications companies. The advantage of cities in attracting further business is heavily dependent on their inherent networking infrastructure.[2]

Hong Kong already has a good networking infrastructure. There is in place a well-established international banking community; a mature stock exchange which is the second largest in Asia; large communities of lawyers, accountants, business consultants and insurance agencies; the world's largest container port; a global hub for aviation; and a centre for the production of Chinese movies and music. This infrastructure will support a steady flow of visitor traffic. In addition, Hong Kong has a unique role to play in serving the People's Republic of China.

Opportunities

New geo-economic opportunities are opening up for Hong Kong which is situated in the middle of the fast-growing Pacific Rim region. Rapid economic growth in this region will stimulate rapid growth in the tourism industry. In fact, short-haul markets are now replacing long-haul markets as the dominant source markets for Hong Kong tourism.

Of even greater importance is the China factor. It has been predicted that the People's Republic of China will sustain its present rapid rate of growth through the next decade and beyond. No city in the world is in a better position to benefit from this growth than Hong Kong is. The growth of the People's Republic of China requires substantial foreign investment. The investment process will lead to substantial China-bound travel through Hong Kong. Cities in the People's Republic of China will emerge to serve as gateways as well. The emergence of a hub necessitates the building of a substantial network in all modes of transport and in business connections. Given Hong Kong's long lead, no city in China will be able to take Hong Kong's place for some time.

Hong Kong will also gain from the outbound traffic from the People's Republic of China. China tourists are bound to increase in number, and they will find Hong Kong a convenient stopover point. True, more international airports will develop within the People's Republic of China, but, at least in the near future, such airports will be unable to build a flight capacity large enough to undermine the importance of Hong Kong.

In addition, the People's Republic of China will actively promote its goods and services to the outside world. China will increasingly use Hong Kong as a platform to show off its products to the world. More China companies will be set up, and more China residents will visit Hong Kong.

A financial centre typically generates a great deal of visitor traffic. The strength of Hong Kong as a financial centre is increasingly seen as dependent on the China factor. If the People's Republic of China is to develop rapidly, it needs a conduit for investment funds. These funds may come through banks, venture capitalists, the stock exchange, or financial institutions. Regardless of the source, Hong Kong is the best place to amass those funds. It already has a high concentration of foreign banks, a well-established stock exchange, and a significant population of venture capitalists and financial institutions.

The liberalization of the People's Republic of China has helped Hong Kong shift towards a service economy. By utilizing China's low-cost facilities, manufacturers in Hong Kong can stay competitive in the world market. Nowadays, manufacturers typically keep two operations, one in Hong Kong and one in China. The one in Hong Kong (the front end) acts as a headquarters, a showroom, a design centre, and an internal control centre. The one in China (the back end) is a labour-intensive, large-scale manufacturing plant. As the front ends of manufacturers by nature maintain worldwide exposure for overseas merchandisers, they generate a great deal of inbound traffic.

Finally, the People's Republic of China, the mainland, has enormous potential as a tourist destination. Much of its varied landscape, culture, and archaeological finds remain unknown to the world. Many places in China would prove amazing not only to westerners but also to ethnic Chinese who reside overseas and have yet to see the site of their ancestral home and the magnificent heritage of China. Moreover, eco-touism — exploration of natural habitats untouched by human civilization — is expected to become increasingly popular among people of the West. This trend bodes well for China's potential as a tourist destination. What this means for tourism in Hong Kong is that, on the one hand, a great deal of China-bound traffic will stop in Hong Kong, while on the other hand it will make Hong Kong much more attractive to tourists.

Constraints

Despite the vast potential that tourism offers, its development in Hong Kong does face a number of restrictions. Foremost among them are several capacity constraints. First, hotel capacity presents a serious problem. Second, airport capacity is a major bottleneck. Although the new Chek Lap Kok airport will provide relief for a few years, continuous expansion will have to take place to handle the rapidly increasing passenger flow. Third, flight capacity poses a major constraint. International aviation regulation imposes constraints on the *flight* capacity that serves Hong Kong. These constraints are quite separate from the constraints imposed by insufficient *airport* capacity. To enhance passenger flow, tight controls over flight capacities have to be relaxed. This argument is developed in full in a subsequent chapter.

One source of the capacity constraint problem is the volatility of the tourism business. It makes perfect business sense to hold back investment in capacity expansion in the face of an uncertain future. A boom could well be a transitory event. Quick expansion on the basis of a transitory boom could lead to heavy future losses. The gains and losses have to be carefully weighed. The tourism business is very sensitive to global economic conditions. The volume of vacation travel and business travel tend to move in unison. The severity of the volatility problem may, however, be somewhat reduced in the future because of Hong Kong's increasing reliance on People's Republic of China tourists. Although the economy of the People's Republic of China is also subject to instability, it is not yet closely linked with that of the rest of the world. The volume of tourism business in Hong Kong may therefore be more stable in the future.

A serious lack of new tourist attractions is another constraint commonly pointed out by tourism developers. Ocean Park, The Peak, Repulse Bay, and Stanley are tourist destinations that are more than a decade old. Repeat visitors will not find them attractive. The argument is therefore that new attractions be created quickly. A number of projects are already on the drawing board. They will be discussed in detail in Chapter 7.

A major consideration is that new attractions need land, and land in Hong Kong is expensive. While the government controls the supply of land and is perfectly capable of making land grants, so far it has largely refrained from granting land for the building of tourist attractions. Without land grants, it is hard for private investors to make profits. They would rather put land to a more lucrative use by developing residential estates. Some innovation is required to resolve this problem. One way forward is for the government to package land leases, which incorporate multi-dimensional, multi-sectoral development.

The human resource constraint is a common problem across many sectors in Hong Kong. The tightness of manpower is most keenly felt in the hotel industry. On a per-room basis, the number of hotel workers is gradually diminishing. The reason is not that hotels now require less workers than before but that hotels have difficulty hiring workers who are committed to their work and who possess the right qualities. Although the shrinking manufacturing sector has released workers from factories, most of these workers have difficulty entering the hotel industry. If tourism is to develop uninhibited, this manpower problem has to be addressed.

Service-Oriented Economy

Since the liberalization of the People's Republic of China in 1978, Hong Kong has been moving towards a service-oriented economy. Manufacturers are not suffering from the "shrinking" of industries due to the growth of the service sector. What has happened is that they are utilizing China's abundant resources to expand their businesses which are getting larger rather than smaller. Less and less manufacturing activity occurs locally, and official statistics correctly reflect the diminishing share of manufacturing in the output of Hong Kong. The activities currently undertaken by manufacturers in Hong Kong are largely those of sourcing, accounting, financing, and internal control — activities commonly classified as services.

The transition to a service-oriented economy generates some benefits, at least in the short term. Jobs in the service sector command higher wages than those in the manufacturing sector. Manufacturers are also reaping significant profits from relocating their factories to the People's Republic of China. The chief area of concern is not the present but the longer term. It is not clear how Hong Kong can maintain its historical high growth rate given its present service orientation.

The Role of Export in Economic Growth

As a growth engine, manufacturing activities are more powerful than service activities. The basic reason for this is that manufacturing is export oriented, while services are largely domestically oriented. There is clear evidence that labour productivity in the service sector has grown rather slowly in Hong Kong. This implies that one cannot expect a rapid increase in income in a service-oriented economy.

While more than 80% of manufactured products in Hong Kong were exported in the past, few of the financial services, construction services, business services (accounting, legal, and consulting), health services were exported. This situation may change somewhat as Hong Kong provides more services to the People's Republic of China. The important point remains, however, that tourism stands out as the foremost sector that is capable of exporting services.

Exports provide a powerful stimulus for growth. Domestic demand is much less powerful in this regard. While this phenomenon has been observed many times throughout the world, its reasons are complex. Simply put, exports represent a direct injection of purchasing power into the economy. Without incomes earned from export, purchasing power has to come from within the economy. At the individual level, a person would be less willing to gear up the buying power if no extra income is expected to be forthcoming through sales. At the national level, even if the capacity to produce more output is in place, the economy would still not grow if there are no significant "goods activities" culminating in more exports. The economy would be trapped in a low-output state.

Overview of the Study

The present monograph is organized into eight chapters. Chapter 1 introduces the issues to be analyzed. Chapter 2 analyzes the source markets. The purposes of tourist visits are discussed. Data are presented to show the increasing reliance on short-haul markets, especially the People's Republic of China. The present institutional constraints on the inflow of China tourists, which is an opaque and complex issue, are discussed. The consequence of direct air links between Taiwan and the People's Republic of China, which some people find worrisome, is expected to be slight for obvious reasons. Also discussed in this chapter are the benefits of the convention business and the marketing concept of the integrated Pearl River Delta. Chapter 3 is an analysis of the economic impact of tourism. Evidence of the role of tourism in the export of services is presented. Receipts from tourism are analyzed in detail. Besides the pecuniary benefits, some unmeasurable benefits of tourism are also discussed.

Factors of growth and constraints are analyzed in the next few chapters. Chapter 4 addresses the strategic importance of the aviation industry and the airport capacity problem. Whether a bottleneck is likely to emerge here is critically discussed. Chapter 5 studies the hotel industry, another key industry in the tourism sector. All hotels are privately owned, mostly by real estate developers. They are keen to maximize their investment returns. There have been complaints, however, that hotel rates in Hong Kong are too high and are impeding the growth of tourism. There is obviously some divergence in objectives, and the government cannot avoid facing these issues. The differences are analyzed in Chapter 5 on the basis of data concerning the financial and operation aspects of the industry. The manpower problems of the industry are also addressed. Chapter 6 studies the retail sector. Shopping accounts for the largest tourist spending item. That Hong Kong may be losing its edge as a shopping paradise has generated much concern. Evidence presented suggests that even though the price gap *vis-à-vis* other cities is getting smaller, retailers still possess some competitive advantages. Hong Kong is still attractive to shoppers because of its variety, its volume, and its proximity to source markets. Chapter 7 discusses the building of new tourist attractions. A number of projects are on the drawing board at the moment. The most challenging task ahead is probably that of financing these projects and determining the extent of government involvement. Some suggestions are made in Chapter 7 in this connection.

Policy issues are addressed in Chapter 8, the last chapter. As in other sectors of the economy, the basic philosophy of minimal government intervention should prevail. Nevertheless, given the strategic importance of tourism to the growth of Hong Kong, a more active stance on the part of the government towards nurturing tourism growth is essential. Chapter 8 discusses this necessary change in government thinking in more specific terms.

Notes

1. A boatload of Taiwanese tourists were burnt to death by suspected pirates operating in the Lake (Zhejiang Province, east China).

2. In economics, the fact that the existence of firms attract more firms of the same industry is known as network externality, see for example Katz and Shapiro (1985). The source of such externality is diverse. Take the banking case as an example. Banks need alliances to provide syndicated loans, to spread risk, to provide temporary credits and offer prospects to workers.

CHAPTER 2

The Source Markets

Introduction

The tourism sector is a major business sector in Hong Kong. In terms of economic contribution, tourism generates the most exports of Hong Kong-produced services. Its importance rivals that of financial, banking, and business services. Hong Kong receives more than 10 million visitors a year. The structure of tourism in Hong Kong has changed over the years. Chief among the changes is the liberalization of China. China's "open policy" has resulted in a steady and expanding stream of outbound tourists departing from China via Hong Kong, and an expanding stream of tourists from all over the world going in the opposite direction.

This chapter provides a systematic analysis of the tourism sector. In a usual manner, this analysis starts with identifying visitors to Hong Kong, defining the purposes of their visit, and determining their expenditures and the length of their stay. Various topics of concern are addressed to, including the supply constraints of tourists from China, the effect of direct air link between PRC and Taiwan, the "Pearl River Delta" concept, and the business convention market .

The largest source market of tourists to Hong Kong is definitely the People's Republic of China. Yet the flow of outbound tourists from China has been restricted by some institutional constraints. There is concern over whether these constraints will tighten, now that the 1997 handover of Hong Kong to China has taken place. A subsequent section of this monograph explains that there are

Table 2.1

Visitor Arrivals by Country of Residence

	1985		1990		1995	
	Arrivals	%	Arrivals	%	Arrivals	%
Japan	635,767	17.4	1,331,677	20.2	1,691,283	16.6
Taiwan	176,617	4.8	1,344,641	20.4	1,761,111	17.3
South & S E Asia	832,890	22.8	988,967	15.0	1,419,699	13.9
Australia, N Z & Pacific	301,856	8.3	311,763	4.7	335,867	3.3
Americas	781,056	21.4	807,692	12.3	986,342	9.7
Europe, Africa, & Mid-East	565,727	15.5	816,093	12.4	1,249,915	12.3
P.R.C.	308,978	8.4	754,376	11.5	2,243,245	22.0
Others	53,926	1.5	225,641	3.4	512,532	5.0
Total	3,656,817	100.0	6,580,850	100.0	10,199,994	100.0

Source: *A Statistical Review of Tourism 1995*, HKTA.

conflicts of interests among various agencies in the People's Republic of China. It is argued, however, that, even taking into consideration the complicating factors, the number of People's Republic of China visitors coming to Hong Kong is likely to grow rather than to diminish in the future.

Another popular area of concern stems from the imminent establishment of direct air links between Taiwan and the People's Republic of China, which would undermine Hong Kong as a stopover point. Statistical data suggest, however, that the impact on Hong Kong of a decrease in stopover traffic, even substantial, would be small. A subsequent section explains the reasons underlying this optimism.

Besides these issues, there are two new aspects of the tourism industry that deserve mention. The first is the emerging marketing concept of the Pearl River Delta, which vastly expands the scope of tourist attractions to visitors in both long-haul and short-haul markets. The second is the growing convention business. Although the number of convention visitors is small relative to that of overall visitors, the convention business has brought significant benefits to the hotel industry and has generally played a part in upgrading the reputation of Hong Kong.

The Source Markets

As a starting point in the analysis, the major source markets are identified. These markets have not changed much in the past decade or so, although their relative importance has been shifting towards countries within Asia. The major markets are Japan, Taiwan, South and Southeast Asia, Australia and New Zealand, the United States and Canada, Europe, and the People's Republic of China. These markets combined account for over 90% of the visitors to Hong Kong.

Table 2.1 sets out the number of tourists coming to Hong Kong from the major markets for 1985, 1990, and 1995. To begin with, one readily notices the dramatic growth in the number of arrivals over these years. While about 3.7 million visitors came to Hong Kong in 1985, almost double that number (6.6 million) came in 1990, and by 1995 the number had increased to more than 10 million. These numbers translate to an annual growth rate of 10.8% in the decade from 1985 to 1995.

Relative to the size of the population in Hong Kong, the large inflow of visitors highlights the business hub nature of the territory.[1] In this regard, Hong Kong's openness is far ahead of that of other countries in Asia. Only Singapore, with a population of 3 million and an arrival number of 7.1 million in 1995, can boast the same level of openness.

The relative ranking of source markets of tourists to Hong Kong has changed somewhat in the past decade. Two factors stand out in driving these changes. First, the liberalization of the People's Republic of China in terms of economic reform and the relaxing of restraints on outbound travel have caused a massive outflow of visitors from China to Hong Kong. In 1985 there were a little over 300,000 visitors from the People's Republic of China. The number increased to 750,000 in 1990 and rose further to 2.2 million in 1995. In terms of relative share of tourism, the People's Republic of China market accounted for a mere 8.4% in 1985, but by 1990 it had accounted for 22%. China is now clearly Hong Kong's single largest source market of tourists.

There is an argument that casts doubt on the accuracy of the figures pertaining to visitor flow from China. In recent years, an increasing number of China outbound travellers have gone to other countries via Hong Kong. Since they stopped over in Hong Kong on the way out as well as on the way back, the same traveller would be counted twice when determining arrival numbers. Nevertheless, the number of such stopover visitors is not believed to be exceedingly large. In 1995, for example, there were an estimated 340,000 such travellers. Compared to an arrival number of 2.2 million in the same year, the general picture reflected by Table 2.1 remains rather accurate.

The second outstanding factor that has driven the changes reflected in Table 2.1 is the liberalization of outbound travel in Taiwan. As is shown in Table 2.1, the number of arrivals to Hong Kong from Taiwan increased tenfold between 1985 and 1995. In 1995 it accounted for 17% of all visitor arrivals. At present, Taiwan is the second largest source market, right after China. In the past decade, there have been some significant policy changes on the part of the Taiwanese government. In July 1987 it abolished the ban on direct travel to Hong Kong. At the same time, travellers were allowed to bring an amount of up to US$5,000 out of Taiwan. Subsequently, in November 1987, Taiwanese were allowed to travel to the People's Republic of China via a third country. On China's side, measures were also taken to facilitate the entry of Taiwanese. These liberalization measures largely explain the eightfold increase in Taiwanese arrivals to Hong Kong between 1985 and 1990.[2]

While the People's Republic of China and the Taiwan markets have loomed large in the past decade, the other two Asian markets, Japan and South and South East Asia, have also been significant. There has been considerable growth in the number of arrivals to Hong Kong from Japan. In 1995 there were 1.7 million arrivals from Japan, accounting for 16.6% of overall visitor flow, a share that has been holding steady in the past decade. Evidently, a great deal of the tourism demand from Japan was derived from the appreciating yen. One should not overlook, however, that government policy changes also played a part in stimulating Japanese outbound travel. For example, from 1989 to 1992 increasingly generous tax exemptions were granted to companies that paid for employee incentive tours.

South and South East Asia accounted for a significant share of arrivals to Hong Kong in the past decade. Although the arrival numbers did not grow as fast as those of the People's Republic of China and Taiwan, in 1995 there were 1.4 million arrivals from this market, accounting for 14% of the total flow. From 1985 to 1995 the number of arrivals from this market grew by 70%, reflecting the growth of purchasing power in this region and the strengthening linkage between these countries and Hong Kong.

Dominance of Short-Haul Markets

It is customary to categorize source markets into short-haul and long-haul markets. In specific terms, short-haul markets refer to the People's Republic of China, Taiwan, Japan, and South and Southeast Asia. Long-haul markets refer to Australia and New Zealand, the United States and Canada, Europe, Africa, and the Middle East. In the past decade or so, long-haul markets have been receding in importance. In 1985 short-haul markets accounted for a combined share of visitors to Hong Kong of about 50%. This share increased to 66% in 1990 and to 70% in 1995. In contrast, long-haul markets have seen their combined share diminish from 50% in 1985 to 25% in 1995.

The shift towards short-haul markets gives rise to some matters of great interest. Visitors from short-haul markets share similar cultures, languages, and reasons for visiting. The potential for repeat visits is high. Compared to long-haul visitors, short-haul visitors spend their money differently. They enjoy different activities and different sights, and they shop for different items. These differences have to be taken into consideration in the strategic planning of tourism development. Tourist attractions that suit the tastes of short-haul visitors have become more important, and creation of new attractions to suit them has become more urgent.

Table 2.2
Visitor Arrivals by Country / Region of Residence, Singapore
(thousands)

Country / Region	1985 Arrivals	%	1990 Arrivals	%	1995 Arrivals	%
America	219.0	7.2	337.1	6.3	425.8	6.0
Canada	31.0		61.1		61.9	
U.S.	176.3		261.4		345.6	
Asia	1960.7	64.7	3427.3	64.4	5231.6	73.3
ASEAN	1008.5		1442.8		2189.9	
Hong Kong	97.7		194.1		279.8	
Japan	377.6		971.6		1179.0	
Korea	30.8		108.4		351.9	
Taiwan	82.8		224.8		563.3	
Europe	468.4	15.5	943.6	17.7	966.0	13.5
Oceania	368.8	12.2	550.7	10.3	426.6	6.0
Australia	300.8		456.6		346.8	
New Zealand	57.5		72.7		66.2	
Others	14.1	0.5	64.2	1.2	87.3	1.2
Total	3031.0	100.0	5322.9	100.0	7137.3	100

Source: *Yearbook of Statistics Singapore, 1995.*
Note: Arrivals of Malaysians by land excluded.

Table 2.3
Mean Length of Stay of Tourists by Country / Region, Hong Kong, 1993–95
(days)

	1993	1994	1995
Japan	2.9	3.0	3.0
Taiwan	2.7	2.8	2.9
South & Southeast Asia	3.7	3.7	3.5
Australia, New Zealand & Pacific	4.5	4.4	4.0
Americas	3.8	3.6	3.5
Europe, Africa, & Middle East	4.0	3.7	3.8
P.R.C.	5.7	6.1	5.9
All Countries	3.8	3.9	3.9

Source: *A Statistical Review of Tourism 1994 & 1995,* HKTA.

A brief comparison with Singapore may be of interest here. Singapore is a city-state that encourages free trade and the free flow of travellers. The Singaporean government has been actively promoting tourism in recent years to diversify the economy from manufacturing. Table 2.2 shows the source markets of tourism to Singapore in the decade 1985–95. The numbers in Table 2.2 exclude the arrivals of Malaysians by land. According to 1995 figures, Singapore received slightly more than 7 million visitors. In the same year, Hong Kong received 10 million. But if one takes away People's Republic of China and Taiwan visitors, then arrival numbers in Hong Kong and Singapore were roughly the same. Singapore's emphasis is predominantly on Asia. In 1995, 73% of all visitors to Singapore came from Asia. The balance was accounted for by the United States (6%), Europe (13.5%) and Oceania (6%). Like Hong Kong, short-haul markets in Singapore have far larger weights than long-haul markets. Singapore is also similar to Hong Kong in terms of the rising importance of short-haul markets during the last decade. In specific terms, the share of Asian markets in tourism to Singapore rose from 65% in 1985 to the aforementioned 73% in 1995.

Length of Stay

Visitors generally came to Hong Kong for a short stay. Table 2.3 shows the average length of stay for visitors from each of the major source markets. For all markets combined, the average length of stay was 3.9 days in 1995, almost the same as it was in the previous two years. Visitors who stayed the longest were, not surprisingly, those from China. People's Republic of China visitors spent on average 5.9 days in Hong Kong in 1995. Many of them have relatives in Hong Kong. A sizable proportion of them came in tour groups, which had itineraries lasting from one week to one-and-a-half weeks.

Visitors who came and went most quickly were those from Japan and Taiwan. In 1995 Japanese visitors spent an average of three days, while Taiwanese visitors spent an average of 2.9 days.

Table 2.4

Percentage of Repeat Visitors from Major Source Markets

(%)

Markets	1993	1994	1995
Japan / South Korea	48	49	48
Taiwan	73	73	78
South & S.E. Asia	69	67	68
Australia, New Zealand, & Pacific	50	51	59
Americas	46	48	49
Europe, Africa & Middle East	34	33	41
P.R.C.	47	44	42
All Countries	54	53	54

Table 2.5

Purpose of Visit by Major Market Areas, 1995

(%)

Markets	Vacation	Visiting Friends / Relatives	Business Meetings	En Route	Others
Japan / South Korea	69	2	26	2	1
Taiwan	48	5	38	5	3
South & South East Asia	54	4	35	5	2
Australia, New Zealand, & Pacific	47	4	30	17	3
Americas	48	3	31	15	3
Europe, Africa, & Middle East	61	3	28	6	2
P.R.C.	48	12	26	14	0
All Countries	55	5	30	8	2

Source: *Visitor Profile Report 1995*, HKTA.

Reasons for their relatively short stays are not hard to come by. Further analysis would show that Japanese visitors typically came to shop. Taiwanese visitors typically made repeated visits. Some of them were passing through Hong Kong on the way to China.[3]

Table 2.4 shows the proportion of repeat visitors from each of the source markets. For all countries combined, slightly more than half (54%) were repeat visitors. Taiwan had the highest proportion of repeat visitors (78% in 1995), primarily due to their business operations in Hong Kong and their China-bound trips. Distance from Hong Kong is a factor affecting the proportion of repeat visitors in the other markets. The South and Southeast Asia market had a relatively high percentage of repeat visitors (68% in 1995), while the North American and the Europe markets had relatively low percentages (49% and 41%, respectively, in 1995). There are factors unique to particular markets, as well. Despite the proximity of the People's Republic of China to Hong Kong, less than half of the People's Republic of China visitors were repeat visitors. Because of institutional restrictions, China visitors had to wait months before they could get permission to travel to Hong Kong. Despite the distance, many Australian visitors did make repeated visits (59% in 1995). Because of the location of Australia, many outbound flights from Australia to Europe and the United States make stopovers in Hong Kong.

Purpose of Visit — Business and Vacation

Hong Kong is not a resort destination. Visitors do not come to Hong Kong entirely for pleasure. Besides vacation, they come too for business reasons, to visit friends and relatives on their way to other countries. Table 2.5 presents some numbers that reflect visitors' purposes in coming to Hong Kong.

Having a good time appears to be the visitors' main reason for coming to Hong Kong. As Table 2.5 shows, for all countries combined, 55% of visitors came to Hong Kong for vacations. A particularly high percentage (70% in 1995) of Japanese visitors come to Hong Kong for this reason. Further analysis, described in a separate chapter, shows that shopping is their major activity. Vacationing is also the main purpose of visitors from Europe, Africa, and the Middle East. They are attracted to Hong Kong by its unique features and by its shopping facilities.

Despite the ties between many people of Hong Kong and those in the People's Republic of China and elsewhere, not many visitors from the mainland came to Hong Kong for the sole purpose of visiting friends and relatives. As Table 2.5 shows in 1995, a mere 5% of all visitors came for that reason. Even among People's Republic of China visitors, only one-eighth of them came solely to visit friends and relatives. Of course, those who used to reside in Hong Kong but have emigrated elsewhere are not counted as visitors when they return to Hong Kong.[4]

To attend business meetings is the second most important reason. In 1995, 30% of all visitors came for business purposes. This is evidence of how the business-hub nature of Hong Kong drives the tourism industry.[5] Among individual source markets, Taiwan had the highest percentage of travellers coming to attend business meetings. Not counting those who were People's Republic of China-bound, almost two out of five visitors from Taiwan came for business. Besides the Taiwanese, people in South and Southeast Asia and people from the United States also used Hong Kong as a business hub. Around one-third of the visitors from these two markets came mainly for business purposes. Reflecting the strong business linkages between the People's Republic of China and Hong Kong, many People's Republic of China visitors also came for business. In 1995 more than one-fourth of all People's Republic of China visitors came for business, which translates to almost 600,000 arrivals in that year.[6]

A significant number of people came to Hong Kong as a stopover point for onward travel. The most significant market in this regard came from Australia and New Zealand and the United States and Canada. In 1995, 17% of visitors from Australia and 15 percent of visitors from the United States stayed in Hong Kong briefly before going on to other countries. The population of *en route* visitors here did not include transit passengers, who merely changed planes at the airport. The Australia and New Zealand *en route* visitors used Hong Kong as a stopover point, because there were few non-stop flights coming out of Australia and New Zealand. On the other hand, most of the United States *en route* visitors are believed to have been China bound.

Of special interest is the number of *en route* Taiwanese visitors to Hong Kong. In 1995 one in twenty or 88,000 Taiwanese visitors belonged to this category. Most of these visitors are believed to have been either travelling through Hong Kong to the People's Republic of China or through Hong Kong to Taiwan on their way home. These are the visitors that Hong Kong may lose when direct flights between Taiwan and the People's Republic of China are opened. The numbers suggest that the impact of such direct air links on Hong Kong tourism would be small.

Travel Arrangements

Visitors to Hong Kong typically make their travel arrangements in a number of ways. One common way is by buying an all-inclusive package that covers transportation, hotel accommodation, meals, and possibly entrance fees to entertainment facilities. All-inclusive packages usually contain a fixed itinerary, which the traveller must follow. The advantage is a sense of security and convenience, particularly if the traveller is a first-time visitor, but a certain amount of flexibility has to be sacrificed. A second method of arranging travel is by buying an airfare-plus-hotel package. With such a package, visitors can explore Hong Kong in their own way and at their own pace. They also have the option of deciding on the spot whether to join a half-day or full-day local tour. A third, more expensive way of arranging visits is by booking transportation and hotels separately. This method is favoured by business travellers.

As a tourist destination, Hong Kong is served by thousands of tourist agencies and wholesalers worldwide. As a tourism developer, the Hong Kong Tourist Association (HKTA) maintains contact with these agencies and keeps them informed of forthcoming events and projects. The all-inclusive and airfare-plus-hotel packages are usually produced by wholesalers and airline companies. Smaller tourist agencies run their businesses by retailing these packages to travellers. In this regard the HKTA has helped promote tourism by lining up local stores and restaurants to provide visitors with shopping and dining discount coupons through packages produced by certain large overseas wholesalers.

Table 2.6
Visitor's Travel Arrangements, 1995
(%)

Country of Residence	All Visitors			Vacation Visitors		
	All-Inclusive Package	Air+Hotel Package	Non-Package	All-Inclusive Package	Air+Hotel Package	Non-Package
Japan / South Korea	55	8	38	76	9	15
Taiwan	14	16	70	28	25	47
South & S. E. Asia	22	19	59	38	24	38
Australia, New Zealand, & Pacific	9	37	54	14	46	40
Americas	20	10	70	37	12	51
Europe, Africa, & Middle East	21	26	53	33	35	32
P.R.C.	22	3	76	40	3	57
All Countries	26	13	61	45	17	38

Source: *A Statistical Review of Tourism 1995, HKTA.*
Note: Based on data of all visitors and subsample of vacation visitors.

Table 2.6 shows the importance of package tours in drawing visitors from all over the world. Generally speaking, and with apparent reasons, vacation visitors rely on package tours to a greater degree than do non-vacation visitors; 62% of vacation visitors came to Hong Kong on package tours, whereas only 39% of visitors overall came on such tours in 1995. This discrepancy highlights the distinct preference for non-package travel among business travellers. This is true not only for the aggregate visitor population but also for each individual source market in Table 2.6. Comparing across various source markets, visitors from Taiwan, the Americas, and the People's Republic of China depended relatively less on package tours than did visitors from other markets. The probable reasons are: many Taiwanese visitors were repeat visitors or shoppers, U.S. visitors had little difficulty exploring Hong Kong on their own, and many visitors from mainland China had family or friendly connections with local residents.

Mode of Transport

Hong Kong is connected with most parts of the world exclusively by air links. The exception is the People's Republic of China, from which there are frequent train, bus, boat, and air connections to Hong Kong. Before the liberalization of China, visitors to Hong Kong arrived predominantly by air. Things changed dramatically after the liberalization, as more and more People's Republic of China visitors began coming to Hong Kong. The modal distribution of visitors in 1995 is depicted in Table 2.7. As is shown, 67% of visitors arrived by air, 10% by sea, and 23% by land. About half of those who arrived by land were People's Republic of China residents. The rest were residents of other countries on their way out of the People's Republic of China. Among visitors arriving by sea, about one-fifth were Taiwanese, and two-fifths were People's Republic of China residents. Again, these were mainly travellers coming out of China.

The People's Republic of China Factor

The situation regarding People's Republic of China visitors coming to Hong Kong is rather complex. There are basically three ways in which People's Republic of China residents, all of whom are classified as People's Republic of China visitors, can come to Hong Kong for a short stay. They may come by obtaining a two-way exit visa, by joining a tour group, or by stopping over in Hong Kong on their way to other countries.

Holders of People's Republic of China passports must obtain an exit visa before they can leave the country. For a short overseas stay, they may apply for a two-way exit visa. There are commonly two reasons to apply for such a visa. The first is for personal reasons, such as to visit relatives, in which case some sort of guarantee is required from a relative residing in Hong Kong. The second is for

Table 2.7

Visitor Arrivals by Mode of Transport, 1995

Country of Residence	Air	Sea	Land	Total
Japan	1,433,887	77,358	180,038	1,691,283
South Korea	281,830	9,899	61,252	352,981
Taiwan	1,139,166	226,149	395,796	1,761,111
South and South East Asia	1,157,065	50,460	212,174	1,419,699
Australia, New Zealand, & Pacific	278,109	16,754	41,004	335,867
Americas	728,647	78,757	178,938	986,342
Europe, Africa, & Middle East	1,027,728	60,012	162,175	1,249,915
P.R.C.	721,518	443,162	1,078,565	2,243,245
Others	55,256	92,056	12,239	159,551
All Countries	6,823,206	1,054,607	2,322,181	10,199,994
Percentage Distribution	66.9	10.3	22.8	100.0

Source: *A Statistical Review of Tourism 1995,* HKTA.

official (or business) reasons, in which case endorsement by the company or unit for which the applicant is working is required. Holders of two-way visas are obliged to go back to the People's Republic of China after the stay overseas. At present, half or more People's Republic of China visitors to Hong Kong are believed to come holding such visas. These visitors usually have accommodation provided by relatives or business associates, and their spending pattern is expected to be somewhat different from that of other visitors.

Many People's Republic of China residents visit Hong Kong by joining tour groups. At present, there are quotas on visitors travelling in this manner. The number of visitors coming in via tour groups is limited to a daily maximum of 22 groups of 48 persons each. In other words, about 385,000 People's Republic of China tourists come to Hong Kong in tour groups in a year. These quotas are filled by a few companies with substantial People's Republic of China interests. Since the number of people wishing to join these tour groups far exceeds the number of quotas, they have to wait from weeks to months to make the trip. According to tour operators, the quotas are set by the Hong Kong government. Since Hong Kong officials want to avoid overloading the infrastructure and since they need resources to process applications, the requirements are posing definite limits to the daily intake.

Most tour groups from China come not by air but by sea and land. In fact, the first tour group that came to Hong Kong by air was authorized by the Hong Kong government only in November 1995. The government was evidently concerned about congestion at the airport.

Group tours usually last eight to ten days. Tourists might not stay with the group throughout the entire stay in Hong Kong. They typically spend three days with the group and the rest of the time with friends and relatives. The demand for hotels is therefore not as large as it is on the part of visitors from other source markets. The companies that sell the tours also run three- to four- star hotels to accommodate their own customers.

More and more People's Republic of China tourists are stopping over in Hong Kong on their way to other countries. At present, a People's Republic of China passport holder can stay in Hong Kong for seven days on producing confirmed onward tickets and an entry visa to another country. What this means is that a People's Republic of China tourist heading for another country can stay in Hong Kong as a stopover point for seven days without an entry visa issued by the Hong Kong government. On the way back to China, the same tourist is allowed to stay in Hong Kong for another seven days. This concession came into effect in June 1993. Before that, stopover People's Republic of China visitors had to obtain a visa from the Immigration Department at the time of entry. The concession greatly facilitated the flow of People's Republic of China visitors at the immigration control points and reduced the workload of the Immigration Department. It also allowed stopover visitors to enter Hong Kong at any immigration control point, eliminating bottlenecks.

According to industry sources, the number of stopover visitors to Hong Kong has been growing since 1993. In 1995 an estimated 340,000 stopover visitors came to Hong Kong, a number comparable to that of tour group participants during the same time period.

The immigration policy of allowing visa-free entry to stopover visitors seems to have aroused conflicts among tourist agencies in China. Visitors can now come to Hong Kong for a seven-day stay without joining a tour group. The agencies that sell Hong Kong tours are not the same as those that sell tours to other countries, though there is some overlap. Some agencies for Hong Kong tours fear that their business will be taken away. Complaints have been lodged against the Hong Kong government for being too lenient on stopover visitors. There has even been concern over the possible restriction of such visa-free entries after the handover in July 1997. Nevertheless, at the moment, there are still only a small number of direct flights out of any People's Republic of China city. Most tourists from China, regardless of their final destination, need to stop over in Hong Kong. If they go by any mode other than by plane, they must enter Hong Kong. Any restriction over stopovers will create a huge workload for the Immigration Department. For this reason, the current policy of visa-free entry is likely to continue for some time.

In fact, the volume of outbound travel from China is set for unprecedented growth, which will bring huge benefits to Hong Kong. At present, for People's Republic of China passport holders, every exit from the country has to be approved by the government. This restriction will soon be liberalized. The People's Republic of China government will soon begin to issue multiple-exit visas that are valid for five years and that can be extended for another five. Holders of a multiple-exit visa can travel freely out of the country. The liberalization will create a huge outflow of tourists. A large proportion of these tourists will travel via Hong Kong, as cities in China do not have sufficient transport connections with the world.

Regional Growth

Hong Kong is going to benefit from the increase in outbound travel from the People's Republic of China as well as from the growth of tourism in the Asia-Pacific region. In the past decade the Asia-Pacific region has been the fastest growth region in the world in terms of passenger traffic. In 1985 the region accounted for 25.2% of world passenger traffic. By 1990 the share had increased to 31.2%. According to the projection of the Pacific Economic Cooperation Council, the share will further increase to 39.2% in 2000 and to 51.1% in 2010.[7] The bulk of the growth will come from traffic within the Asia-Pacific region — in other words, from short-haul flights.[8]

To accommodate traffic growth, aircraft capacity has to expand quickly. It is projected that fleet capacity in the region will increase by 50% in the next two decades. Financing the expansion will not be too difficult, as many of the airlines in the region are making healthy profits. In 1992, for example, five of the ten most profitable airline companies in the world came from the region. Four of the five most profitable airlines were also from the region.

Along with the expansion of fleet capacity, major airport expansion programmes are being planned in many cities of the region. By 2000 a number of cities will have significantly expanded airport capacities. Bangkok will have an airport capable of annually handling 25 million passengers in the beginning. Guangzhou will have an airport capable of handling 45 million; Hong Kong's 35 million; Kuala Lumpur's 25 million; and Seoul's 40 million. Finally, Shanghai will have a second airport capable of handling 60 million. With these expansions, the six cities will have an airport capacity of 230 million passengers, as compared to 75 million at present.

There will also be vast expansion in hotel capacity in the region. It is estimated that there will be as many as 200,000 additional rooms by 2000, distributed across hotels of different standards. From a regional point of view, a severe room shortage is unlikely to develop, despite fast growth in passenger traffic,

All projections suggest that the region is going to experience rapid growth in tourism. As a major centrally-located business hub of the region, Hong Kong will probably receive a fair share of the expansion.

Direct Air Links between China and Taiwan

Some members of the tourism sector have expressed concern over the establishment of direct air links between Taiwan and the People's Republic of China, fearing that it will mean a loss of business for them. This fear is not unfounded given the lifting of restrictions by the Taiwanese government over People's Republic of China-bound travel in 1987 and the generally welcoming attitude towards Taiwanese tourists on the part of the mainland government. Moreover, there is substantial Taiwanese direct investment in certain coastal cities of southern China. A great deal of trading in raw materials and consumer goods is also taking place between Taiwan and the People's Republic of China. At present, the flow of tourists, capital, and goods has to be channelled through Hong Kong for purely political reasons. The Taiwanese government prohibits any form of direct contact, whether it is commodity trade, investment, or transport, with the People's Republic of China. Since Hong Kong became part of the People's Republic of China in 1997, however, direct contact between Taiwan and the People's Republic of China is now inevitable. It would therefore be natural to create air links between Taiwan and other cities in the mainland.

Some authors believe that direct air links between Taiwan and China would have a serious negative impact on Hong Kong tourism. Hobson and Ko (1994) describe the situation as follows. "If there is political rapprochement and the establishment of direct airlinks between China and Taiwan, then Hong Kong may lose a substantial number of tourist arrivals.... To what extent Taiwanese tourist arrivals would decline is not exactly clear. However, it is currently estimated that 45% are stopping over on their way to China, and therefore the hotel industry can be expected to lose hundreds of thousands of room nights."

Subsequent evidence produced by the HKTA suggests that the impact may not be quite as drastic. As is shown in Table 2.5, only 5% of Taiwanese arrivals in 1995 were passing through Hong Kong. Assuming that they were all mainland-bound or mainland-originated, and that all of them would have been lost if direct air links were established, Hong Kong would have lost 88,000 arrivals in 1995 — less than 1% of total arrivals. Clearly, Hobson and Ko's (1994) *assumption* that 45% of Taiwanese arrivals were stopping over in Hong Kong has been the reason for their pessimistic outlook.[9]

Table 2.5 shows that a far larger number of Taiwanese arrivals were in Hong Kong for business meetings. One could defend the pessimistic stance by arguing that as Taiwan and the People's Republic of China set up more direct links, not only in air transport but also in trade and investment, Taiwanese would no longer find it necessary to set up operations in Hong Kong, and thus the number of business visitors would diminish gradually. This view is some-what overly pessimistic. It is based on the assumption that Hong Kong has no value as a business hub. In fact, Hong Kong has advan-tages over other cities in that it possesses a wide range of infrastructures that support business activities. Telecommunica-tions, management expertise, financing mechanisms, sourcing capabilities, logistics, and internal control are but a few aspects of Hong Kong's fortes. Hong Kong is a place where business people come together and close deals. The hub nature of Hong Kong is in itself a driving force behind tourism development.

Pearl River Delta Concept

There is an emerging marketing concept that envisages Hong Kong as the heart of the Pearl River Delta. The HKTA is the major driving force behind this conceptual initiative, marketing the region under the brand name PRIDE.

Geographically, the Pearl River Delta is a triangle with Hong Kong situated at the eastern end, Macau to the west, and the vast Guangdong province to the north. The Pearl River Delta Tourism Marketing Organisation was established in December 1993. It is the product of a collaborative effort between the HKTA, the Macau Government Tourist Office, and the Guangdong Provincial Tourism Bureau, with the endorsement of the China National

Tourism Administration. The expenditure needed to create the organization was shared by the three members.

The principal work of the organization involves the design of itineraries that cover the attractions of the Pearl River Delta. The organization produces promotional brochures, videos, and pamphlets in various languages to promote the region to travel agencies around the world. It also participates in travel trade shows as a distinct entity. The target consumer group is that of vacation travellers. Interestingly, although it originally targeted long-haul source markets, expecting that PRIDE would offer long-haul visitors convenient excursions around Hong Kong, short-haul markets have brought the greatest success to the scheme.

PRIDE's philosophy is that Hong Kong, Macau, and Guangdong can complement each other as tourist destinations. Hong Kong can attract vacationers with its shopping opportunities and its excellent restaurants, but it is relatively weak when it comes to historical spots and natural scenery. Macau, on the other hand, has a distinct Portuguese heritage, together with historical buildings and a large number of casinos. Guangdong is relatively unexplored and has considerable potential when it comes to natural scenery, temples, handicraft factories, and historical sites. As facilities in Guangdong are relatively cheap, a number of theme parks have been built in Shenzhen, and they have proven popular with vacationers. These theme parks include the Splendid China Park and the China Folk Culture Villages. Because the region is rather compact, and because there are well-established transport links — coaches, ferries, and trains — the visitor can tour the region in a single day.

The PRIDE concept is extremely beneficial to Hong Kong tourism. By marketing Hong Kong, Macau, and Guangdong together as a single destination, the scope of activities on offer to tourists becomes much broader. The major advantage comes from the fact that, while both Macau and Guangdong have their own international airports, their international flight capacities are still limited. Visitors coming to the Pearl River Delta have to reach Hong

Kong first. The PRIDE initiative is therefore best seen as an expansion of the range of tourist attractions offered by Hong Kong.

Convention and Exhibition Business

The convention business refers to the organization of international conferences and exhibitions in Hong Kong. Organizers could be multinational corporations, multilateral institutions, charitable organizations, learned societies, or trade associations. These conferences and exhibitions bring to Hong Kong much more than just tourism receipts. The major benefit is on the non-pecuniary side. Many trade exhibitions are showcases for Hong Kong exports. There are regular trade fairs for fashion clothing, watches and clocks, toys, leather goods, and jewellery. International conferences are prestigious events that promote and symbolize the international stature of Hong Kong. They strengthen the role of Hong Kong as a conduit for the transfer of knowledge in a global context. They also broaden the exposure of local participants in international events. This is a vital aspect of the role of Hong Kong as a business centre in the future.

In 1995, 268 conventions, 63 exhibitions, and 351 corporate meetings were held in Hong Kong. In addition, 1,493 business groups came to Hong Kong through incentive rewards for corporate employees. Altogether, these events brought more than 340,000 visitors. In comparison, in 1994 Singapore held 642 conventions and 96 exhibitions and received 3,348 incentive groups, bringing in a total of 380,000 visitors. Both Hong Kong and Singapore appear to be popular venues for international events.

The Hong Kong government does not, as a rule, provide direct subsidy to the organization of conferences. The HKTA, however, does provide information support for organizations in the process of bidding for the events. In contrast, some cities in Asia do offer direct subsidy to the organization of conferences in the form of reduced hotel rates and venue rentals. The support that the Hong Kong government provides is mainly indirect. One example of such indirect support is the Hong Kong Convention and Exhibition Centre, which was built by the Trade Development Council on land granted by the government. The venue, one of the best in Hong Kong, is, however, run by a private company on commercial principles. If it had been necessary to build the centre on land acquired on the market, it would have been hard for it to break even. Also it would charge rates so high that the convention business would not flourish.

In terms of monetary receipts, the hotel industry is the largest beneficiary of the convention and exhibition business. There is evidence that convention and exhibition visitors spend much more than does the typical visitor during a stay in Hong Kong, and more than half of their expenditure goes to hotel bills. While the typical visitor spends a good deal on shopping, convention and exhibition visitors spend only one-fifth of their money on shopping. The major reason for this spending difference is that convention and exhibition visitors stay twice as long as typical visitors.

Summing Up

Hong Kong already has a vibrant tourism sector. It received more than 10 million visitors in 1995, and the number is still growing. The composition of visitors has changed significantly over the years, gradually shifting towards short-haul source markets. China, in particular, has emerged rapidly to become the largest source market. In the future, as China continues to grow and tourism travel within the Asia-Pacific region surges ahead, Hong Kong tourism is set for large gains. Even if direct air links between Taiwan and the People's Republic of China are to be established, the impact on Hong Kong is not likely to be large. At present, about 30% of visitors to Hong Kong are business travellers, a significant proportion of which are conference participants. Business travellers constitute a stabilizing factor in an otherwise volatile business. It is clear, however, that short-haul and repeat visitors will play an increasingly important role in Hong Kong tourism in the future. This brings up the question of how the attractiveness of Hong Kong as a tourist destination can be sustained. Even though, as is explained in Chapter 7, shopping will continue to play a significant role in the future, more tourist attractions have to be planned. The development of these attractions has to leverage on the unique cultural and locational strengths of Hong Kong. In this regard, China will provide abundant fresh resources, and the Pearl River Delta initiative is clearly a valuable step in the right direction.

Notes

1. Over 30% of visitors came to Hong Kong on business.

2. Taiwanese visitors exhibited two remarkable features. First, almost 80% of them were repeat visitors, the highest among all source markets. Second, half of them came for vacation (with shopping being the main activity) and the rest mainly for business (resulting from Taiwanese trade and investment in the PRC conducted through Hong Kong).

3. The average length of stay for visitors in Singapore was 3.4 days in 1995, not significantly different from the Hong Kong average.

4. That returning emigrants are not counted as visitors may seem odd. There is a technical difficulty involved. Most returning emigrants clear immigration check by showing their Hong Kong identification cards rather than their foreign passports. Tourism statistics count them as Hong Kong residents, not visitors.

5. The term "business hub" refers to Hong Kong's function as a business centre. This meaning should be identified as separate from that of an "aviation hub", as used in the hub-and-spoke aviation literature.

6. For comparison, in Singapore in 1995, 56% of visitors were holiday travellers, 14% were pure business travellers, and 3% were business-cum-holiday travellers. In addition, 10% were in transit, and the rest unspecified. Source: *Yearbook of Statistics, Singapore 1995*.

7. Predictions according to *Pacific Economic Development Report 1995*, p. 98, Fig. 17-1. It should be emphasized that these forecasts are at best long-term averages. Transitory downturns, which worry investors in tourism, are not predictable.

8. By "Asia Pacific region", the Americas are not included.

9. The source of the "45%" estimate was not cited by Hobson and Ko (1994). Their estimate is likely to be a gross exaggeration.

CHAPTER 3

The Economic Impact
of Tourism

Introduction

Hong Kong has always been well known for its openness to world trade. It has also captured a large share of the global revenue that international travel generates. Since 1990 Hong Kong's level of international visitor spending has been one of the highest in the Asia-Pacific region (excluding the United States). Visitor spending in Hong Kong was twice that in Japan, an economic superpower.

This evidence suggests the significant role that tourism plays in Hong Kong's economy. Tourism is in fact Hong Kong's largest sector in the export of services, ahead of shipping, insurance, finance, and trade-related services by a wide margin. In the past, Hong Kong's growth has always been export led. The manufacturing sector, which exported most of its output, was the engine of growth. As Hong Kong is transforming into a service-oriented economy, manufacturing can no longer be the growth engine. Development of the tourism sector is a critical issue in the future development of the Hong Kong economy.

Tourism generates less tangible benefits that are often overlooked. The development of tourism has led to the creation of new commercial complexes and recreational facilities that are popular among local residents as well as tourists. Furthermore, the tourism business quietly forces sector participants to match their service quality with the world standard. The outwardly oriented nature of tourism prevents its workers from becoming complacent and from compromising service standards, a problem frequently observed in inwardly oriented service industries. In addition, the ability to provide world-class service is an asset in itself. The knowledge necessary to run tourism facilities of all kinds can be transferred to other places. At the moment, the People's Republic of China and many other countries in the region are developing tourism. There are good opportunities for Hong Kong to transfer such "knowledge" technology to them.

International Visitor Spending

According to statistics compiled by the World Tourism Organization and cited by the Pacific Economic Cooperation Council, among countries in the Pacific Rim, Hong Kong amassed the second largest amount of money generated by international visitor spending. It was second only to the United States in this regard. Table 3.1 shows that from 1990 to 1993, visitor spending in Hong Kong increased sharply from US$5 billion to US$7.6 billion. In the same period, Australia, Malaysia, New Zealand, Papua New Guinea, Singapore, Thailand, Canada, Mexico, and the United States experienced only modest increases in visitor spending. There was no growth in Japan or the Republic of Korea. Besides Hong Kong, only the People's Republic of China, Indonesia, the Philippines, and Chile experienced rapid growth in visitor spending during this period. As a result, by 1993 Hong Kong had become the second largest tourism centre in the Pacific Rim. It is a remarkable fact that, despite being just a city, Hong Kong has amassed more money from visitor spending than Japan, Australia, the Republic of Korea, Thailand, or Mexico.

One could argue that visitor spending does not measure the degree to which a country is exposed externally, and that the statistics just cited has not controlled for the overall size of the economy. A large economy should by itself attract more business-related visitors, even if it is not outwardly oriented. As is shown in the second block of Table 3.1, there was a great deal of variation in the economy size of countries in the region during the period. In 1993 the United States had a Gross Domestic Product (GDP) of US$6,260 billion, Japan US$4,166 billion, Hong Kong US$116 billion, Singapore US$55 billion, and Papua New Guinea US$5 billion. The third block of Table 3.1 normalizes the visitor spending in each country by the size of the economy. The results show that, at 10.5% in 1993, Singapore was the most tourism-oriented country in the group. The GDP of Singapore was merely about eight to ten times the volume of international visitor spending. Hong Kong was the second most tourism-oriented economy, with GDP standing at around fifteen times as much as international visitor spending. This evidence suggests that, controlling for the size of the respective economies, Singapore is in fact more outwardly oriented than Hong Kong, although Hong Kong is more tourism oriented than other countries. From another angle, one could also argue that Singapore is more dependent on tourism than Hong Kong. The success of the tourism sector in Singapore is a result of many factors, among which are its central location in Southeast Asia, its "open skies" aviation policy, its adequate infrastructure, its business centre status, and its encouragement of foreign direct investment. Regardless of the reasons, if we use Singapore as a benchmark, we find that there is room for further tourism development in Hong Kong.[1]

Visitor spending divided by GDP is different from tourism's share in the GDP. Visitor spending does not indicate the contribution of tourism to the economy. Visitor spending may go partly towards the purchase of imported goods and services and may therefore constitute a leak in the economy. Estimating the net gain derived from visitor spending is generally a complex matter. The case for Hong Kong is discussed in a following section.

Dominant Exporter of Services

As a small, open economy, Hong Kong's well-being is critically dependent on export. The purchase of Hong Kong exports injects money into the economy, which then generates buying power. Exports can be generated in a number of ways. Goods may be

Table 3.1
Visitor Spending in Asia-Pacific Countries, 1990–93

	International Visitor Spending (US$ million)				Gross Domestic Product (US$ million)				IVS divided by GDP (%)			
	1990	1991	1992	1993	1990	1991	1992	1993	1990	1991	1992	1993
Australia	4,088	4,484	4,405	4,655	293,312	294,320	278,135	288,129	1.4	1.5	1.6	1.6
P.R.C.	2,218	2,845	3,948	4,683	338,568	371,550	423,505	541,034	0.7	0.8	0.9	0.9
Hong Kong	**5,032**	**5,078**	**6,037**	**7,562**	**74,676**	**85,916**	**100,650**	**116,178**	**6.7**	**5.9**	**6.0**	**6.5**
Indonesia	2,105	2,522	3,278	3,988	102,892	114,208	126,472	141,245	2.0	2.2	2.6	2.8
Japan	3,578	3,435	3,588	3,557	3,158,757	3,604,609	3,712,585	4,166,044	0.1	0.1	0.1	0.1
Rep. of Korea	3,559	3,426	3,272	3,510	250,613	283,562	304,911	328,608	1.4	1.2	1.1	1.1
Malaysia	1,667	1,530	1,768	1,876	42,883	47,562	56,579	60,362	3.9	3.2	3.1	3.1
New Zealand	1,019	1,021	1,032	1,165	42,989	39,453	39,152	45,176	2.4	2.6	2.6	2.6
P.N.Guinea	41	41	49	45	3,228	3,784	4,195	5,075	1.3	1.1	1.2	0.9
Philippines	1,306	1,281	1,674	2,122	38,464	46,829	53,873	53,251	3.4	2.7	3.1	4.0
Singapore	4,593	4,557	5,250	5,793	37,944	44,809	48,075	55,353	12.1	10.2	10.9	10.5
Thailand	4,326	3,923	4,829	5,014	86,635	99,684	111,011	123,767	5.0	3.9	4.4	4.1
Canada	5,612	5,886	5,712	5,897	571,387	577,348	536,069	532,348	1.0	1.0	1.1	1.1
Chile	540	700	706	824	27,500	32,087	40,563	43,070	2.0	2.1	1.7	1.9
Mexico	5,467	5,881	6,085	6,167	233,075	281,721	327,127	363,168	2.3	2.1	1.9	1.7
U.S.	43,007	48,384	53,861	56,501	5,490,000	5,656,000	5,937,000	6,260,000	0.8	0.9	0.9	0.9

Source: *Sourcebook on Travel and Tourism in the APEC Region*, American Express Travel Related Services and Pacific Economic Cooperation Council, November 1995. *Monthly Bulletin of Statistics*, Statistics Division, United Nations, January 1996.

Note: IVS stands for International Visitor Spending.

manufactured in whole or in part in Hong Kong and then exported from Hong Kong. These goods are classified as domestic exports. Alternatively, goods may be manufactured outside Hong Kong, but instead of being exported directly to foreign markets, they are shipped to Hong Kong where they are repackaged. These goods are then exported to foreign markets as re-exports. A third way in which Hong Kong can export is by providing services to foreign people and businesses. There are many ways in which services can be rendered to foreigners, and there are difficulties in measuring all such services accurately. In any case, according to the most reliable statistics, tourism-related services account for the lion's share of export of services.

Tourism comprises a number of exportable services. A visitor may come to Hong Kong via flights run by a Hong Kong airline, namely Cathay Pacific or Dragonair.[2] While in Hong Kong, the visitor is typically accommodated in a local hotel. The visitor then shops, has meals, and travels around the city. All payments for hotel, dining, shopping, and domestic travelling constitute purchases of services that Hong Kong, in effect, "exports".

Tourism is not the only service exporter. Shipping, for example, is also a sector that generates considerable export revenues. When a shipping company transports goods for a forwarder situated outside Hong Kong, the fee received for the shipment is export revenues. Similarly, when a Hong Kong airline (Cathay Pacific or Dragonair) flies a passenger on one of its flights, a service is exported. When an insurance company issues an insurance policy to an insuree situated outside Hong Kong, Hong Kong is also exporting a service. When a bank undertakes a financial service for a foreign business, say, undertaking a remittance or closing a loan deal, a service is exported. All these services are service exports.

Increasing rather rapidly in recent years has been the export of trade-related services. Most manufacturing facilities have been moved out of Hong Kong; manufacturers engage in support services for manufacturing plants outside Hong Kong. Manufacturers source materials, provide market information, arrange financing, and co-ordinate between buyers and producers.

Table 3.2
Share of Tourism in the Export of Services, 1990–93
(HK$ million)

Item of Service Export	1990	1991	1992	1993
Transportation				
Shipping	22,682	27,299	31,196	33,124
Air transportation	19,669	22,379	24,639	26,649
Others[1]	12,101	15,018	17,637	20,317
Travel	41,457	42,651	53,232	61,563
Insurance	1,319	1,478	2,327	3,506
Financial	6,104	7,665	9,231	13,821
Others	11,226	12,818	15,228	16,767
Subtotal	114,558	129,308	153,490	175,747
Trade-related services	27,763	31,779	35,862	42,455
Total export of services	142,321	161,087	189,352	218,202
Total tourism export[2]	61,126	65,030	77,871	88,212
Share of tourism in total export of services	42.9%	40.4%	41.1%	40.4%

Source: *Annual Digest of Statistics 1995*, Census and Statistics Department, Hong Kong.

Correspondence with the National Income Branch (1), Census and Statistics Department

Notes: 1. "Others" under "Transportation" includes expenditure of foreign airlines and shipping companies on fuel oils and port charges.

      2. Tourism = air transportation + travel.

As the consumers of these services are located outside Hong Kong, such services are also in effect exports.

Across the range of exportable services, tourism is by far the most important.[3] Table 3.2 presents government estimates of the magnitude of service exports from 1990 to 1993. Tourism is not treated by the Census and Statistics Department as a separate sector. The best we can do is to combine different sectors in the statistics to arrive at an estimate for tourism.[4]

Table 3.2 shows that financial services were not exported on a large scale between 1990 and 1993. In 1993 financial exports stood at $13.8 billion, surpassing only the insurance sector, although the figure was already twice what it had been in 1990. The data suggest that the importance of the financial sector as an exporter is relatively minor. This is true despite the size of the financial sector in terms of economic output and employment. It appears that the financial sector is still very domestically oriented.

Tourism export stood at $88 billion in 1993, more than six times the value of financial export. More importantly, tourism accounted for 40% of all service exports. Tourism was by far the largest service exporter. Even though tourism receipts have always been subject to external shocks (such as movements in exchange rates, political events, and the Gulf War), the share of tourism in service exports has been stable. From 1990 to 1993 the share of tourism in service exports had always been above 40%.

As the largest service exporter in Hong Kong, tourism plays a critical role in driving the future growth of the economy. The growth performance of Hong Kong has been outstanding by Asian and world standards in the last three decades. Much of this growth has been attributed to the rapid development of manufacture exports. But as manufacturing facilities moved into the People's Republic of China and elsewhere, domestic exports of goods stagnated. Initially, re-exports were expanding rapidly, as goods manufactured in the People's Republic of China had to be shipped back to Hong Kong for repackaging before export. At the moment, however, there are signs that even re-exports are becoming stagnant. The reason is that, increasingly manufactured goods are either exported directly or they merely pass through Hong Kong as a transshipment point. These changes have led to concern over what will fuel the growth of Hong Kong's economy in the future. The above analysis suggests that tourism has an important role to play in continuing the drive towards export-led growth.

One might ask why export is so important in driving growth and why other sources of demand, such as private consumption and investment, and, for that matter, government expenditure, cannot play an equally effective role. One explanation is based on observations in the region. Most of the fast-growing economies in Asia are export oriented, while many of the slow-growing economies are

inwardly oriented. A traditional view is that exports force developing economies to catch up with global best practice. Combining
cheap labour in developing economies with modern technology can
bring about rapid growth.

A newer theory, which utilizes the concept of co-ordination
failure, suggests that exports have a stimulating effect on the
economy that internal demand does not have. This theory is of
particular relevance to the present discussion. Simply put, the
theory goes as follows. For the economy to grow, it is essential to
make people work harder, learn more skills, and invest more in
machinery and technology. For a number of reasons, these goals are
hard to achieve in a closed and inwardly oriented economy. The
main reason for the difficulty is that to start off a growth process,
the economy needs an initial push. Without the prospect of extra
business, firms do not start investing, and workers cannot earn
extra pay even if they are willing to work more. If workers do not
earn more, the demand for the firm's output cannot increase, thus
confirming the stagnant expectations of the firms. Of critical
importance therefore is extra demand from outside the economy.
The government is not a good candidate to stimulate the economy.
Even though it can stimulate demand in the short run, it easily runs
into problems of inefficiencies in the longer run. Expansionary
government policy is generally not a desirable engine for long-term
growth. What this boils down to is the conclusion that among the
different ways to stimulate growth in Hong Kong, export
promotion is a promising course to take.

Estimate of Contribution to GDP and Growth

While tourist spending is an important indicator of the strength of
the tourism sector, it does not by itself indicate the contribution of
the sector to the output of the economy. In economics, the output of
the economy is commonly measured by the GDP, which by
definition is the value of goods and services produced by the
economy within the geographical boundaries of the country. Since
the money that a visitor spends in Hong Kong may consist of

substantial import content, not all tourism spending is counted as a contribution to the output of the economy. To bring up a separate matter, the portion of tourist spending that is retained in Hong Kong could trigger further spending in other parts of the economy. The indirect benefit of tourist spending should therefore be taken into consideration in a comprehensive model of measurement.

The GDP is the key concept used around the world to measure the output of an economy. The GDP's rate of increase from one year to the next is used to measure the growth rate of the economy. Thus, in discussing growth issues, it is important to understand what the GDP actually measures.

A simple example can clarify the meaning of GDP. Consider a shirt. Suppose it is made of imported fabric that costs the manufacturer $10. The manufacturer expends effort through design and machining and sells the shirt to a shop for $40. A tourist comes along and buys the shirt for $100. As the tourist pays $100, the entire amount is recorded as visitor spending, which is also the value of the service exported. The shop, which adds value ($60) to the shirt, is contributing $60 to the GDP. This is a contribution made by the service sector to the GDP. The manufacturer, which adds a value of $30 to the shirt, is contributing another $30 to the GDP. In total, the amount added to the GDP is $90. Looked at from another angle, the tourist who makes a contribution of $90 to the GDP is making a purchase of $100, the difference of $10 being the cost of importing the fabric. The value that the manufacturer and the shop add to the shirt is an output of the economy. This value actually adds to the income of the people involved in the process. The manufacturing value added of $30 adds to the profit of the manufacturer and the wages of the workers. The retail value added of $60 similarly adds to the profit of the shop and the wages of its employees. The point to note here is that while there is an export of tourism service (or visitor spending) of $100, the addition to the GDP is only $90. There is a leakage of $10 due to the import content of the shirt.

A further complication in measuring the impact of tourism on economic output arises from the indirect ripple effects that tourism

Table 3.3a

Aggregate and Average Visitor Spending by Spending Items, 1995

(HK$ million)

Country / Region	Shopping	Hotel Bills	Meals Outside Hotels	Tours	Others	Total	per capita (HK$)	per diem (HK$)
Japan	7,580.9	4,030.0	1239.4	728.4	531.9	14,110.6	8,343	2,800
Taiwan	9,332.2	2,850.3	1,702.8	258.2	976.9	15,120.3	8,586	2,940
South & South East Asia	5,143.2	2,976.6	1,183.5	246.3	532.9	10,082.4	7,102	2,047
Australia, New Zealand & Pacific	798.6	937.1	234.0	56.2	127.8	2,153.7	6,412	1,587
Americas	1,813.8	3,388.1	766.0	144.7	397.0	6,509.5	6,600	1,870
Europe, Africa & Middle East	2,501.0	3,598.5	1,022.7	234.9	490.3	7,847.5	6,278	1,643
P.R.C.	8,386.4	2,566.6	1,783.4	346.3	663.6	13,746.3	6,128	1,048
Others	1,512.2	1,064.6	421.8	123.8	246.9	3,369.4	6,574	n.a.
Total	37,068.4	21,411.9	8,353.6	2,138.7	3,967.1	72,939.6	7,151	1,848

Source: *A Statistical Review of Tourism 1995*, HKTA.

Note: n.a. not available.

spending generates. When the profit of a firm increases, the firm does not keep the extra profit in a safe. Instead, it invests to expand the business. The amount of money that it spends on investment gives rise to further business in other firms in the economy. Similarly, when workers receive more wages, they spend on consumption and purchase assets, again giving rise to extra demand for goods and services. These ripple effects could go on and on in stimulating the economy. The cumulative impact could be several times that of the initial one. Economists elsewhere in the world believe that the manufacturing sector has the strongest ripple effect on the economy, as it is closely linked to sectors such as financing, transport, and warehousing. Whether this is the case in Hong Kong is unclear. Whether the manufacturing sector stimulates the economy more than tourism and other services sectors in Hong Kong is still a pending issue.

Visitor Spending and Spending Patterns

Visitor spending in Hong Kong exceeded that of all but one Asia-Pacific country in 1993. It might be interesting to explore in greater depth the question of where visitors actually spent their money. Knowing the breakdown of visitor spending can help identify Hong Kong's strengths as a tourism centre.

Statistics on spending patterns have been collected systematically by the HKTA. The statistics are based on face-to-face surveys of visitors identified at the airport, seaport, and train station.

Table 3.3a shows the total visitor spending of each of the major source markets in 1995 and its breakdown into individual items. The major source markets are Japan; Taiwan; South and Southeast Asia; Australia, New Zealand, and the Pacific; the Americas; Europe, Africa, and the Middle East; and the People's Republic of China. The individual spending items are shopping, hotel bills, meals eaten outside hotels, and tours. These four items accounted for over 90% of visitor spending in 1995. The items included under "shopping" need no elaboration. "Hotel Bills" are all expenditures incurred inside hotels, including such items as room charges, long-distance telephone call charges, meals, and miscellaneous hotel charges. Expenditures on meals taken outside hotels are reflected in the item "Meals Outside Hotels". The item "Tours" reflects the amount paid for half-day or full-day tours organized by local tourist agencies.

Table 3.3a shows that in 1995 total visitor spending amounted to $73 billion. The largest source markets were, in descending order, Taiwan, Japan, the People's Republic of China, and South and Southeast Asia, each of which brought over $10 billion in revenue to Hong Kong. All four markets are short-haul markets.

That Taiwan was the largest market in revenue terms is not surprising, as the number of Taiwanese arrivals to Hong Kong was one of the highest among all markets. But, in fact, Taiwanese visitors also brought the highest revenue per capita, as is shown in the "Per Capita Spending" column in Table 3.3a. On average, each Taiwanese visitor spent HK$8,586 in 1995, more than visitors from any other market. It appears that Taiwanese were the heaviest spenders. Furthermore, as Taiwanese made the shortest stays, one would expect them to have been the quickest spenders, too. This was indeed the case, as is shown in the last column of Table 3.3a. Taiwanese spent HK$2,940 per day, more than visitors from any other market.

Japanese visitors were a close second in terms of both per capita spending and per diem spending. A distant third were visitors from South and Southeast Asia. As for the other four markets — the three long-haul markets and the People's Republic of China — spending was relatively low.

Not only did visitors from short-haul markets (except the People's Republic of China) spend more than long-haul visitors, but they also spent their money differently. Table 3.3b shows that in 1995 visitors from the three short-haul markets spent more than half the money on shopping. Visitors from Taiwan spent 62% on shopping, those from Japan spent 54%, and those from South and Southeast Asia spent 51%. In contrast, among long-haul visitors, those from Australia, New Zealand, and the Pacific spent only 37%

Table 3.3b
Spending Breakdown across Items by Country / Region, 1995
(%)

Country / Region	Shopping	Hotel Bills	Meals Outside Hotels	Tours	Others
Japan	53.7	28.6	8.8	5.2	3.8
Taiwan	61.7	18.9	11.3	1.7	6.5
South & Southeast Asia	51.0	29.5	11.7	2.4	5.3
Australia, New Zealand, & Pacific	37.1	43.5	10.9	2.6	5.9
Americas	27.9	52.0	11.8	2.2	6.1
Europe	31.9	45.9	13.0	3.0	6.2
P.R.C.	61.0	18.7	13.0	2.5	4.8
Others	44.9	31.6	12.5	3.7	7.3
Total	50.8	29.4	11.5	2.9	5.4

Source: *A Statistical Review of Tourism 1995,* HKTA.

on shopping; those from Europe spent 32%; and those from the Americas spent a mere 28%. The overall picture reflected by the data is that short-haul visitors (except those from the People's Republic of China) spent more on a per person and per diem basis, and that they spent a much larger proportion on shopping. Shopping is therefore a major source of tourism revenue in Hong Kong. As the last row of Table 3.3b shows, in 1995 more than half of tourism revenue came from "shopping", about 30% from "hotel bills", and about 11% from "meals outside hotels".

The foregoing analysis hints that the shopping sector might have been biased towards the short-haul markets during the period under discussion. This was indeed the case, as is made clear in Table 3.3c. In 1995 over 80% of the shopping revenue came from the four short-haul markets, with Taiwan accounting for 25%, the People's Republic of China accounting for 23%, Japan accounting for 21%, and South and Southeast Asia accounting for 14%. In contrast, patronage for the hotel sector was much more diversified. Although long-haul visitors spent relatively less, the bulk of their spending was on hotel bills, and so they did account for a sizeable proportion of hotel revenue. In 1995 the three long-haul markets accounted for 37% of hotel revenue.

Chapter 3

Table 3.3c
Breakdown of Spending Items across Visitor Markets, 1995
(%)

Country / Region	Shopping	Hotel Bills	Meals Outside Hotels	Tours	Other	Total
Japan	20.5	18.8	14.8	34.1	13.4	19.4
Taiwan	25.2	13.3	20.4	12.1	24.6	20.7
South & South East Asia	13.9	13.9	14.2	11.5	13.4	13.8
Australia, New Zealand, & Pacific	2.2	4.4	2.8	2.6	3.2	3.0
Americas	4.9	15.8	9.2	6.8	10.0	8.9
Europe, Africa, & Middle East	6.8	16.8	12.2	11.0	12.4	10.8
P.R.C.	22.6	12.0	21.4	16.2	16.7	18.9
Other	4.1	5.0	5.1	5.8	6.2	4.6
Total	100.0	100.0	100.0	100.0	100.0	100.0

Source: *A Statistical Review of Tourism 1995*, HKTA.

On the whole, the analysis of spending patterns clearly shows that the tourism sector is heavily dependent on the four short-haul markets, namely, Taiwan, Japan, South and Southeast Asia, and the People's Republic of China. The sector is particularly reliant on these markets in the shopping category. The central role played by retailing in tourism business is therefore firmly established. For the future development of the tourism sector, the appeal of Hong Kong shopping, particularly in comparison to shopping in other Asian countries, is a matter that calls for serious attention.

Intangible Benefits

The impact of tourism is not limited to tangible economic benefits. Indeed, tourism brings a number of important intangible benefits that have a far-reaching and profound influence on the territory. To provide a balanced assessment of the role that tourism plays, some of these intangible benefits should be discussed as well.

One principal benefit of tourism development is that it opens the economy to outside influences. Because visitors are generally well travelled, they expect tourism services to meet international standards. Even though service provision is a localized matter, because of the quality standards that visitors demand, service providers are in effect operating and competing in a global market. If one travels to an underdeveloped country where tourism has not been actively developed, one finds a whole range of poorly run services. Such services may include those provided by hotels, restaurants, retail shops, and transport modes. There, the service providers are not customer friendly, and the technology used is not up to date. It is also interesting to note that when these economies begin to develop, the pace of development goes hand in hand with the opening up of the country to tourists. The best service is offered by businesses that operate in tourist districts.

It is amazing how quickly tourism-related businesses can catch up with world standards. Take hotel services as an example. Tourism cannot develop without the support of world-class hotels. An underdeveloped economy does not have the knowledge necessary to build and run such hotels. What usually happens is that new hotels are built by joint ventures with the participation of foreign investors. More importantly, these hotels are managed by hotel chains that manage dozens of hotels around the world. Very quickly, therefore, the best-practice technology is transferred and adapted to the local environment. Success is so evident that one can expect the same, if not better, service from a hotel in an underdeveloped country as from a hotel run by the same management company in the developed world.

Another illustration of the influence of tourism business on service standards can be found in the airline industry. Many countries have two aviation sectors, a domestic one and an international one. Flights in the two sectors may be operated by a single company or by different companies. One general observation is that services provided on international flights are usually better than those provided on domestic flights. One minor reason for this may be that international flights can earn more profit than domestic flights can. But the major reason is that with international flights, airline companies are competing directly or indirectly against airline companies in nearby countries. They may not undercut prices to draw passengers, but they are clearly conscious that passengers may choose other airlines travelling the same route. Airlines cannot avoid an international comparison of service quality. It is amazing to find how well run many airlines of developing countries are, despite the fact that other sectors in domestic economies are still in infancy.

Hong Kong has already achieved world standards in both hotel management and airline services. Yet the continued development of tourism would still be a major advantage in maintaining service standards in airport management, shopping mall management, retailing, restaurants, theme parks, tour agencies, and other related businesses. The maintenance and improvement of service quality against world standards is an important factor in the future success of Hong Kong as a service-oriented economy.

Another intangible benefit that tourism brings to Hong Kong is the upgrading of social amenities. In Hong Kong, visitors and residents mingle freely. There is no district, and, without exaggeration, no building in which only visitors can be found. Places in Hong Kong that visitors frequent, such as hotels, shopping centres, the Peak, Ocean Park and Repulse Bay, see more resident customers than visitors. As these tourist attractions are upgraded, the major beneficiaries are the residents. In the hotels of Hong Kong, local residents account for a large proportion of food and beverage revenue. The development of hotels also creates modern and sophisticated neighbourhoods for local residents. One prime example is the development of the Pacific Place area in Wanchai. Developed on a former site of British barracks, the area consists of office buildings, a large multi-storeyed shopping centre, three luxury hotels, an apartment block, Hong Kong Park, and direct access to the Mass Transit Railway. This is a modern complex that local residents thoroughly appreciate. Another example of such a complex is the Gold Coast Development. This project was undertaken by a private real estate developer and consists of a luxury hotel, a yacht club, a shopping centre, and apartment blocks. Other areas that draw tourists, such as Ocean Park, The Peak, and Repulse Bay, have upgraded their facilities, benefiting not only visitors but also local residents.

The development of tourism has helped Hong Kong acquire a great deal of management know-how. This is valuable "soft" technology that can be transferred to other countries. It is well known that, in service industries in general and tourist industries in particular, management experience is critical. The ability to manage facilities well is more important than acquiring the capital to set up the facilities. Building a hotel is one thing; managing it so that money can be made is quite another. And the same applies to the management of shopping centres. In the retail business, the art of merchandising (i.e., buying goods that consumers like), the training of workers, the layout of stores, the keeping of stock, and the prevention of theft, are just some of the most important prerequisites for success. Every service business has its own set of requisite skills. The skills that Hong Kong has can be transferred to other countries. While many Asian countries are promising candidates in this regard, the People's Republic of China is the brightest prospect.

In the hotel business, the transfer of technology to China has been limited so far. New hotels developed in China are mostly managed by international hotel chains. The old hotels are, as they were in the past, managed by the government. Some hotel workers in the People's Republic of China have been recruited from Hong Kong; therefore, the extent of the technology transfer was limited to exporting workers to the People's Republic of China. The management of People's Republic of China hotels by Hong Kong companies is not common. One reason for this is that the management companies usually have global customer networks. Hong Kong does not have management companies that possess these networks. But things could change rapidly in this regard. As the tourism industry in the People's Republic of China develops, a large number of medium-tariff hotels will have to be built. These hotels, which may be owned by the state or by People's Republic of China interests, will create a niche for the participation of Hong Kong management.

Besides hotel management, other tourism-related industries in China will gradually open to Hong Kong businesses. Many Hong Kong companies are already managing shopping centres, department stores, and smaller retail shops in the People's Republic of China. Tourist agencies, in charge of selling overseas tours and issuing air tickets, will gradually be opened to Hong Kong companies too. Looking further into the future, the management of theme parks, art galleries, and museums may also occupy a niche into which Hong Kong businesses can tap.

Notes

1. One feature that is common between Hong Kong and Singapore is that both cities have no domestic tourism, whereas domestic tourism involving tourists going from one city to another is substantial in U.S. and Japan.

2. There is no Hong Kong airline, other than Cathay Pacific and Dragonair, which runs regular or chartered flights to Hong Kong.

3. There is a subtle distinction between an export of goods and an export of services. If a good is shipped out of Hong Kong and subsequently bought by a consumer, this is an export of a good. By contrast, if the consumer comes to Hong Kong, buys the good and brings it home afterwards, this is an export of a service. From the point of view of economic development, the two ways of exporting make little difference. What is being emphasized is the export nature of tourism.

4. First, air transportation is definitely one component of tourism. But placing all air transportation export in the tourism category yields a slight overestimate, because air transportation export includes flights not involving Hong Kong. The slight overestimate would be balanced out by failing to include "shipping" and "others" under transportation, which includes transport services consumed by visitors who did not arrive by air. In the end, the estimate of the export of tourism services is reasonably accurate. Having settled the transportation issue, the rest of tourism export is assumed to be "travel", as is indicated in Table 3.2. "Travel" items include hotel bills, shopping expenditures, and payments for other locally provided services.

CHAPTER 4

Air Service

Introduction

With the exception of tourists from the People's Republic of China, most visitors to Hong Kong arrive by air. If Hong Kong is to develop its full potential in tourism, then its air service link with other countries must develop at a rapid pace. The foremost requirement in this regard is airport capacity. As a result of a delay in the government's decision to build a replacement airport, the Kai Tak Airport has been operating above design capacity for quite many years. The Civil Aviation Department has run out of ways to squeeze enough room out of the existing capacity to accommodate traffic growth. The midnight curfew for noise control and the saturation of the single runway have severely constrained the traffic volume that Kai Tak can handle. Shortage of available flights serving Hong Kong has seriously limited the growth of tourism in recent years.

The airport capacity problem will be alleviated to a significant degree when the new Chek Lap Kok Airport opens in 1998. The new airport offers a much larger capacity and has a great deal of expansion potential. The next challenge is to determine how the extra capacity can be put to good use. Air service in the international aviation business is governed by Air Services Agreements which are treaties negotiated between sovereign states. The Sino-British Joint Declaration allows the Hong Kong government to negotiate and sign Air Services Agreements with other sovereign states. These agreements will continue to be effective after the transition of sovereignty. Accordingly, since 1984 the Hong Kong government has been actively negotiating many such agreements. By the end of 1996 fifteen agreements had been signed and a few more were close to completion. After the transition, the Basic Law allows the Hong Kong Special Administrative Region government to continue the negotiation and signing of Air Services Agreements, with the exception of routes that connect Hong Kong with cities in the mainland.

If tourism in Hong Kong is to develop rapidly, the government must take steps to liberalize the access of foreign carriers to the new airport. This calls for a drastic change in government thinking. In the aviation industry, the primary objective of most governments is to protect their own carriers. The Air Services Agreements that are in force in Asia are mostly bilateral, involving only two sovereign states. Most of these agreements allow governments to designate airlines to run routes and allow airlines to share route markets in a fair and mutually acceptable manner. The result has been frequently high airfare and inadequate service. The structure of the agreements jeopardizes the competitiveness of Asian countries. As Asia is unlikely to follow in the footsteps of Europe in launching a sweeping liberalization of its regional aviation industry, the Hong Kong government should seriously consider ways in which appropriate policies can capture the growing Asian aviation market to further the interests of Hong Kong.

New Airport

A new airport in Hong Kong is long overdue. Congestion at the Kai Tak Airport has been a continuous problem ever since it began operation in the late 1950s. Over the years, more space has been added, mainly in the passenger terminal, the baggage-handling facilities, and the apron area. As an extra runway could not be built to supplement the existing runway, the limits of expansion would be reached soon. There is a limit to the number of take-offs and landings that a runway at any airport can handle. When that limit is reached, the airport is saturated, no matter how large the other facilities such as the passenger terminal are. The only way in which expansion can occur is to construct a second runway. Due to safety reasons, the second runway must not be too close to the first. In Hong Kong, the geographical limitations of the airport preclude the construction of a second runway, and therefore building a replacement airport was the only solution. The government understood the situation well, but the problem was that a new airport would cost well over HK$100 billion, making it far more costly than any other project the government had ever attempted. It was only in late 1989 that the government finally decided to build a new airport at Chek Lap Kok on Lantau Island. The new airport, together with the supporting infrastructure, will cost an estimated HK$160 billion. It is reportedly one of the largest civil engineering projects ever to take place anywhere in the world. The new airport will commence operation in April 1998.

At the time of its opening, the new airport will have only one runway. Construction of a second runway will start immediately afterwards, so that by the time Phase One is completed, two runways will be operating together. Unlike Kai Tak Airport, which has to be closed down for several hours at night for noise control reasons, the new airport will operate twenty-four hours a day throughout the year. Even with only one runway, the new airport can easily handle 35 million passengers in one year. As a comparison, the Kai Tak Airport, stretched to the limits, handled 27.4 million passengers in 1995. The new airport is much larger in terms of various facilities. Table 4.1 provides a comparison of the two airports. The site of the new airport is almost four times as large as that of the old. The taxiway system, the area which prepares an aircraft for take-off and for parking after landing, is twenty-six kilometres in length, almost four times as long. Perhaps the biggest difference is in the passenger area. At the new airport, the passenger area spans 515,000 square metres, eight times the size of Kai Tak's passenger area, and has seats for almost 10,000 people. To keep a large volume of travellers informed and to allow them to flow efficiently and comfortably through the airport, there will be 2,000 flight information display boards, 120 frontal gates (as opposed to remote gates requiring shuttle buses for access), 288 check-in

Chapter 4

Table 4.1
Capacities of Hong Kong's Old and New Airports

	Existing Kai Tak Airport	New Airport at Opening	At Completion of Phase I
Total airport site	333.8 hectares	1,248 hectares	1,248 hectares
Annual passengers (millions)	27.4	35	35
	(1995 actual)	(design capacity)	(design capacity)
Runways	1	1	2
Runway length	3,393 m	3,800 m	3,800 m
Taxiway system	7.1 km	26 km	35 km
Apron area	1.03 sq km	1.25 sq km	1.33 sq m
Passenger area	66,000 sq km	515,000 sq km	550,000 sq m
Retail area	13,600 sq m	30,000 sq m	31,300 sq m
Retail outlets	40	120	120
Aircraft gates (frontal)	8	38	48
Aircraft gates (remote)	56	27	27
Check in counters	200	288	288
Immigration desks (arrivals)	90	124	124
Immigration desks (departures)	76	100	100
Baggage claim units	6	12	12
Travelators	0	1	1
Automated people mover	0	1	1
Carparking spaces	1,732	3,100	3,100
Taxi loadng spaces	15	24	24
Bus stops	6	10	10
Lounge seating	3,812	9,446	9,446
Luggage trolleys	3,500	5,600	5,600
Flight info display boards	283	2,000	2,000

Source: *Airport Authority Annual Report 1995 / 96.*

Note: The name of new airport is Chek Lap Kok.

counters, 224 immigration desks, 12 baggage claim units, travelators, and an automatic people mover. There will also be 120 retail outlets occupying an area of 30,000 square metres, an area twice as large as that at Kai Tak. When Phase One is completed, further expansion will occur in the taxiway system, the passenger area, and the number of departure gates.

Despite its many drawbacks, one big advantage of the Kai Tak Airport is its proximity to business and hotel districts. Under good traffic conditions, it takes just minutes to reach Hong Kong's urban core from Kai Tak. The new airport, on the other hand, would be almost an hour away from downtown Hong Kong. For this reason, a rail link connecting the new airport and Central is being built. A special express service will take 23 minutes from the airport to Central. For departing passengers, there will be check-in facilities at the rail station at Central so that they do not have to carry their baggage with them to the airport. The Airport Authority believes that, eventually, up to half of all travellers to the airport will go by train. The remainder will go by bus, taxi, and private car.

The new airport will greatly increase the competitiveness of Hong Kong tourism. The added capacity will allow for more flights to Hong Kong, and the modern design of the terminal will allow passengers to access the business district rapidly and comfortably. Yet flights will not come by themselves from other countries; flight numbers are governed by Air Services Agreements that regulate flight service between Hong Kong and other countries. If Hong Kong is to put the added capacity of the airport to good use, the government has to devise innovative ways to maximize traffic growth within the framework of the Air Services Agreements. This is going to be a big challenge.

Bilateral Air Services Agreements

For most countries, there are two aviation industries — a domestic industry and an international industry. In Hong Kong, and in some small countries, there is only an international industry. Flight service in the international industry is governed by Air Services Agreements, treaties negotiated among sovereign states. Most of these agreements are bilateral, involving only two sovereign states. In Asia, most flight service is governed by Bilateral Air Services Agreements (BASA).

Before the Sino-British Joint Declaration came into effect in 1984, air service connecting Hong Kong with the rest of the world was negotiated and signed by the U.K. government. In those negotiations, the Hong Kong government acted as an observer only. The Joint Declaration specifically allowed the Hong Kong government to negotiate and sign BASAs with other countries as a contracting party. The Basic Law, which sets down the legal framework of the Special Administrative Region, further allows the government to negotiate and sign BASAs after 1997. The only exceptions are flights that involve one or more cities in mainland

Table 4.2

Effective Air Services Agreements between Hong Kong and Foreign Countries at the end of 1996

Foreign Country	Effective Date
Netherlands	17 September 1986
Switzerland	26 January 1988
Canada	24 June 1988
Brunei	9 January 1989
France	20 August 1990
New Zealand	22 February 1991
Malaysia	4 March 1991
Brazil	6 September 1991
Sri Lanka	24 February 1993
Australia	15 September 1993
Germany	5 May 1995
Republic of Korea	29 March 1996
Singapore	30 April 1996
Italy	9 October 1996
India	10 October 1996

Source: *Hong Kong Government Gazette Special Supplement,* various issues.

China. What this means is that the Hong Kong government has been given the authority to regulate flight service connecting Hong Kong and all other countries besides China.

The Hong Kong government has been actively negotiating BASAs in the last ten years. By the end of 1996 fifteen BASAs had been signed with countries; they are the Netherlands, Switzerland, Canada, Brunei, France, New Zealand, Malaysia, Brazil, Sri Lanka, Australia, Germany, the Republic of Korea, Singapore, Italy, and India (see Table 4.2). BASAs with Japan, the Philippines, and the United States are close to being officially signed by the end of 1996. The contractual structure of the post-1997 aviation industry is solidly in place.

In aviation jargons, there are five basic "freedoms". One principal objective of establishing a BASA with another country is to establish the freedoms on a reciprocal basis. The first freedom grants the right to fly across the area of another country without landing. This freedom can be economically important if it results in considerably shorter flight distances. The second freedom grants the right to make stops for non-traffic purposes. This freedom is frequently used for refuelling stop-overs on long-haul flights. The third freedom grants one country the right to carry passengers, for a reward, from a point at home to a point in the other country. The fourth freedom grants one country the right to carry passengers, for a reward, from a point in the other country back to a point at home. The third and fourth freedoms establish an air market between two countries. The fifth freedom grants one country the right to carry passengers from a third country to the other country or from the other country to a third country. In practice, the first, second, third, and fourth freedoms are usually conferred in a BASA, whereas the fifth freedom is usually very restricted.

The fifteen BASAs that the Hong Kong government has signed so far are similar in content. The salient features are as follows. First, the first, second, third, and fourth freedoms has been firmly established. Second, Hong Kong cannot carry passengers between two points in the other country. The restriction applies to the other country as well, although this carries little meaning, as Hong Kong has only one airport. Third, each contracting party, either Hong Kong or the other country, has the right to designate one or more airlines to operate air service. The airline that Hong Kong designates must have "its principal place of business in Hong Kong". The airline that the other country designates must be substantially owned or effectively controlled by the government or nationals of the other country. The condition for designation imposed on other countries is quite common among BASAs in general. The "place of principal business" condition for a Hong Kong designated airline is a bit unusual. This provision is, however, essential, because Cathay Pacific, the principal Hong Kong airline, is 44% owned by Swire Pacific (a U.K. company), 25% owned by CITIC (a Hong Kong company controlled ultimately by the Chinese government) and 31% owned by China National Aviation Corporation, China Travel Service, and the Hong Kong public combined. Cathay Pacific is neither owned nor controlled by the Hong Kong government; nor is it by the Hong Kong people.

Another Hong Kong airline, Dragonair, is fully qualified to operate Hong Kong air service because an airline only has to be based in Hong Kong in order to qualify for designation. Dragonair started operation in the mid-1980s as a Hong Kong-based airline aiming to compete with Cathay Pacific on China routes. The government refused to grant Dragonair designation to run those routes, and Dragonair's plans were thwarted. It was subsequently acquired and controlled by Swire Pacific and Cathay Pacific. In May 1996 China National Aviation Corporation, which was directly controlled by the Chinese government, bought a large volume of shares in Dragonair from Swire Pacific and Cathay Pacific and became the largest shareholder of Dragonair. In the same restructuring deal, Swire Pacific placed new shares in Cathay Pacific with CITIC and reduced its shareholding of Cathay Pacific to 44%, as is mentioned above. Consequently, both Cathay Pacific and Dragonair are majority owned by companies controlled by the Chinese government. Since then, all flights that serve China have been run by Dragonair.

The fourth salient feature that is common across Hong Kong BASAs is that operating airlines are allowed to form an economic cartel. In the BASA between Hong Kong and Switzerland, signed on 26 January 1988, one finds the following provisions in Article 7: Principles Governing Operation of Agreed Services.

1. There shall be fair and equal opportunity for the designated airlines of both Contracting Parties to operate the agreed services on the specified routes.
2. In operating the agreed services the designated airlines of each Contracting Party shall take into account the interests of the designated airlines of the other Contracting Party so as not to affect unduly the services which the latter provide on the whole or part of the same routes.
3. The agreed services provided by the designated airlines of the Contracting Parties shall bear a close relationship to the requirements of the public for transportation on the specified routes and shall have as their primary objective

the provision at a reasonable load factor of capacity adequate to meet the current and reasonably anticipated requirements for the carriage of passengers and cargo, including mail, to or from the area of the Contracting Party which has designated the airline.

One finds exactly the same wording in the other fourteen Hong Kong BASAs. These principles allow airlines to fix airfares, to equate their supply of service, and generally to avoid competing against each other. To ensure that there is "fair and equal opportunity" and a "reasonable load factor", an airline cannot increase service without the consent of the airline of the other country. A strong airline cannot increase supply if the other airline in the same market fears a reduction in business.

A fifth salient feature also common across all fifteen BASAs is that while the fifth freedom is not ruled out, its existence in reality is subject to severe restriction. The following provision in the Notes to Section 1 of the Annex to the Hong Kong–Switzerland BASA is typical. "No traffic may be picked up at an intermediate point or at a point beyond and set down at a point in Switzerland or vice versa, except as may from time to time be agreed by the aeronautical authorities of the Contracting Parties. This restriction also applies to all forms of stopover traffic." The same paragraph, with "Hong Kong" replacing "Switzerland" is found in the Notes to Section 2 of the Annex. This provision specifically rules out fifth-freedom traffic by either country unless a mutual agreement is reached.

In practice, most governments act to protect their own airlines. The battle for air rights is therefore fought without the interests of travellers or the development of the economy uppermost in mind. On third- and fourth-freedom flights, the basic concern of most governments is whether the airlines of both contracting countries are sharing the market evenly, even though this is not required by the BASAs. On fifth-freedom flights, the overriding concern is whether such flights will take business away from the country's own airline. Little consideration is given to the fact that allowing more access to a country has the potential of reducing airfare and

Table 4.3

Scheduled Air Services Provided by Airlines

Carrier	Incoming Flights per week	Seat Capacity per week	Share (%)
Aeroflot Soviet Airlines	2	350	0.09
Air China	36	10,518	2.74
Air France	11	2,750	0.72
Air India	7	2,744	0.72
Air Lanka	3	876	0.23
Air Mauritius	2	508	0.13
Air New Zealand	3	1,071	0.28
Air Niugini	2	418	0.11
Alitalia	6	1,698	0.44
All Nippon Airways	11	3,861	1.01
Ansett Australia Airline	5	2,070	0.54
Asiana Airlines	7	1,904	0.50
Biman Bangladesh Airlines	2	548	0.14
British Airways	15	6,015	1.57
British Asia Airways	6	2,406	0.63
Canadian Airlines International	14	5,978	1.56
Cathay Pacific Airways	357	129,855	33.85
China Airlines	126	38,069	9.92
China Eastern Airlines	63	14,364	3.74
China Southern Airlines	83	15,676	4.09
Continental Micronesia Airlines	2	574	0.15
Emirates	11	1,991	0.52
Garuda Indonesia	17	5,709	1.49
Gulf Air	7	1,400	0.36
Hong Kong Dragon Airlines	66	14,184	3.70
JAL–Japan Airlines	56	17,986	4.69
Japan Asia Airways	7	1,848	0.48
KLM–Royal Dutch Airlines	4	1,136	0.30
Korean Airlines	14	3,612	0.94
Lauda Air	2	574	0.15
Lufthansa–German Airlines	7	2,709	0.71
Malaysian Airlines	15	4,307	1.12
Myanmar Airways	2	292	0.08
Northwest Airlines	10	3,600	0.94
Philippine Airlines	28	9,159	2.39
Qantas Airways	31	8,228	2.14
Royal Air Cambodge	2	290	0.08
Royal Brunei Airlines	2	357	0.09
Royal Nepal Airlines	3	564	0.15
Scandinavian Airlines System	4	768	0.20
Singapore Airlines	37	14,541	3.79
South African Airways	2	664	0.17
Swissair	7	1,759	0.46
Thai International	67	24,727	6.45
United Airlines	42	16,107	4.20
Varig Brazilian Airlines	2	538	0.14
Vietnam Airlines	14	2,575	0.67
Virgin Atlantic Airways	7	1,771	0.46
Total	1,229	383,649	100.00

Source: *A Statistical Review of Tourism 1995*, HKTA.

enhancing a country's status as a business centre. In Hong Kong in particular, one often hears the argument that a lot of traffic originates in Hong Kong, by virtue of its business activities and its central location. Since airlines of other countries want a slice of the business, they want to open fifth-freedom rights with Hong Kong, knowing well that Hong Kong, on its part, stands to gain little from the fifth-freedom flights they open. The argument goes on to point out the fact that it is usually locationally deprived cities that push for open-skies agreements (that is to say, agreements with unlimited fifth freedom). This type of argument, which has dominated government thinking, is logically sound. The problem is that it focuses attention exclusively on airline profits. It misses the fact that increased air service to Hong Kong would provide a big boost for Hong Kong's tourism industry and would increase Hong Kong's competitiveness as a business hub.[1]

In light of tourism development, Hong Kong should liberalize fifth-freedom flights to foreign airlines. With Kai Tak Airport's limited capacity, nothing much can be done. The situation will be different when the new airport begins operation. The new airport's much larger capacity creates the potential for a boom in visitor arrivals.

Market Share of Airlines

Hong Kong has been well served by international airlines. By the end of 1995 forty-eight airlines were maintaining scheduled passenger service to Hong Kong. A few more airlines supplied cargo service. Table 4.3 sets out the share of each airline in terms of seat capacity. Of course, seat capacity is not the same as the number of passengers actually carried; this number is regarded as top secret among airlines because it allows for the calculation of load factors. Nevertheless, shares in terms of seat capacity do provide an indication of the dominance of a few individual airlines in the industry.

The 48 airlines serving Hong Kong come from a large number of countries. Direct flights connect each of these countries with Hong Kong, establishing its international hub status. These countries are Russia, the People's Republic of China, France, India, Sri Lanka, Mauritius, New Zealand, Papua New Guinea, Italy, Japan, Australia, the Republic of Korea, Bangladesh, the United Kingdom, Canada, Taiwan, the Pacific Islands, the United Arab Emirates, Indonesia, Saudi Arabia, the Netherlands, Austria, Germany, Malaysia, Burma, the United States, the Philippines, Cambodia, Brunei, Nepal, Denmark, Singapore, South Africa, Switzerland, Thailand, Brazil, and Vietnam.

Let us take a look at the total number of incoming flights that airlines run regularly. By the end of 1995 there were 1,229 incoming flights to Hong Kong per week, not including chartered flights and cargo flights. This frequency translates to 176 landings per day. The single runway therefore has to handle roughly 350 operations per day, all crammed into around sixteen hours because of the midnight curfew. The peak hours are between one and three o'clock in the afternoon, during which time there are typically 50 operations (landings and departures). It is no exaggeration to say that the runway is saturated.

In total, in 1995 there was a capacity of 383,649 seats per week arriving in Hong Kong. If we extrapolate the number to a yearly figure, we get a capacity of 20 million seats, or 40 million seats counting both departures and arrivals. As the airport handled 27.4 million passengers in 1995, we estimate the average load factor to be around 69%. In other words, on average, there were only three vacant seats out of every ten seats coming to and departing from Hong Kong. This is a relatively low vacancy level. It indicates that flights to and from Hong Kong were rather heavily booked. Some potential visitors might have been turned away because they could not book their flights easily.

Looking at the breakdown into capacities of individual airlines, one finds a very uneven picture. This is not surprising, as capacities are governed by BASAs, which grant flights to foreign airlines on a reciprocal basis only. As is explained above, Hong Kong has two designated airlines, Cathay Pacific Airways and Hong Kong Dragon Airlines (Dragonair), which operate on different routes and so do not compete against each other. In the absence of fifth-freedom flights, Cathay Pacific and Dragonair combined would have roughly a 50% share of the capacity coming to and departing from Hong Kong.[2] The reason for this is that the "fair and equal opportunity" principle requires an equal number of seats to be carried by Hong Kong airlines and foreign airlines. Table 4.3 shows that in 1995 Cathay Pacific and Dragonair combined accounted for 38% of all incoming capacities, or 144,039 seats. Third and fourth freedoms would allow foreign airlines to carry roughly the same number of seats to Hong Kong. Third- and fourth-freedom traffic would therefore carry a total of 288,078 seats to Hong Kong. Out of a total of 383,649 seats, we estimate that 95,571 seats, or 25% of the total, were carried by fifth-freedom flights. This percentage has not increased much over the years. It shows that Hong Kong has been rather conservative in granting foreign airlines fifth-freedom rights. A more liberal fifth-freedom policy would probably make access to Hong Kong easier and airfares lower. On both counts, the competitiveness of Hong Kong tourism would be enhanced.

Regional Trends

The source markets of visitors to Hong Kong are increasingly dominated by countries in Asia. Short-haul markets have been displacing long-haul markets. Aviation trends developing in Asia will therefore surely impact the development of tourism in Hong Kong.

There are two prominent trends developing in the Asian aviation industry. First, air traffic is growing rapidly, and a larger share of world air traffic will be accounted for by Asia. Second, the structure of the industry may undergo profound changes, giving rise to huge challenges for the airlines as well as for the governments in the region.

Today the growth of air traffic in the Asia-Pacific region (excluding North America) is twice that within North America and within Europe. This rapid growth has led to a continuous shift in the distribution of world traffic towards the Asia-Pacific region. In 1985 the region accounted for a mere 25.2% of world traffic. This share increased to 31.2% in 1990 and is predicted to increase to 39.2% in 2000 and to 51.1% in 2010. By 2010 the volume of traffic will have quadrupled compared to what it was in 1990. This rapid growth will come about mainly due to three factors. First, most countries in the region will be growing rapidly. As incomes increase, there will be increased demand for travel. Growth in the People's Republic of China will be particularly significant. Second, the aircraft fleet size will expand rapidly in the next decade. The Asia-Pacific region is at present the largest buyer of passenger planes. Third, many cities are putting forward plans to expand airport capacities. These cities include Osaka, Tokyo, Hokkaido, Singapore, Bangkok, Guangzhou (together with increased utilization of airports in Shenzhen, Zhuhai, and Macau), Taipei, and Seoul. The income factor will drive a strong demand-side effect on air traffic, whereas the fleet size and airport capacity factors will drive a strong supply-side effect. These factors will join forces to make the Asia-Pacific region the highest traffic growth area in the next decade.

In the next decade, the market environment of the aviation industry in the Asia-Pacific region could experience drastic changes towards liberalization. Several forces have been at work here. First, airfares in the region tend to be higher, on a distance basis, than are those in the United States, where the domestic industry has been deregulated since 1978. This is intriguing, as airlines in the Asia-Pacific region enjoy cost advantages, relative to their U.S. domestic counterparts, by virtue of lower wage rates. Cost differences between Asian and U.S. airlines should make Asian airfares lower, not higher. Observers have thus been led to believe that the rigid network of Bilateral Air Services Agreements in force in the region has pushed up airfares. Every route market in the region is strongly protected against entry. Strong economic regulation has allowed airlines to form cartels, which fix airfares. Serving as confirming evidence is the uniformly high profitability of Asian airlines. In 1992, for example, four out of the five highest-profit airlines in the world were Asian airlines, namely, Singapore Airlines, Cathay Pacific, China Airways, and Thai Airways. Only the third highest-profit airline, British Airways, was not from Asia. On the other hand, among the ten highest-loss airlines, only one, Japan Airlines. was from Asia (Table 4.4).

As a separate development, the aviation market in the European Union was quickly deregulated according to the Treaty of Rome. The result is that any airline designated by a European Union country can run a service between any two European Union countries. In effect, for routes involving only cities in the European Union, unlimited fifth-freedom rights are granted to all European Union airlines. It is believed that the sweeping liberalization in the European Union will in time lower European Union airfares substantially. This development has forced governments in Asia to consider whether similar changes would benefit Asian countries as well. Liberalization is, of course, not a new concept in Asia. When it was raised in the past, there was concern over the hardship that it might create for weaker airlines, which would in turn cast a burden on the respective governments. This concern has greatly diminished in the last few years, as many airlines have been completely or partially privatized. These privatized airlines include Singapore Airlines, Thai International, Philippine Airlines, Air New Zealand, Malaysian Airlines, and Qantas.

It is unlikely that Asia will follow the European Union's path of liberalization. There is no top-down pressure for liberalization. Yet some degree of liberalization in fifth-freedom rights over specific cities is possible. A number of cities, such as Seoul, Singapore, and Bangkok, are aspiring to become air hubs. They have shown their commitment by substantially expanding their airports. It is unlikely that they will be able to achieve hub status without some relaxation of fifth-freedom rights. For Hong Kong, the threat of these developments is that a great deal of traffic could be diverted elsewhere. The diversion is not limited to transit traffic, which by

Table 4.4
Most and Least Profitable Airlines, 1992

Ten Most Profitable Airlines	Net Profit (US$ million)
Singapore Airlines	518.5
Cathay Pacific	391.5
British Airways	309.8
China Airways	143.3
Thai Airways	120.4
Qantas	106.6
Southwest Airlines	103.6
Swissair	80.4
Air New Zealand	61.8
Malaysian Airline System	57.5

Ten Least Profitable Airlines	Net Profit (US$ million)
Delta Airlines	−468.4
American Airlines	−475.0
Iberia Group	−418.4
United Airlines	−417.0
Northwest Airlines	−405.1
USAir Group	−404.5
Varig	−380.3
Air Canada	−373.9
TAP–Air Portugal	−370.0
Japan Airlines	−349.3

Source: La Croix and Wolff (1996).

itself makes a relatively small contribution to the economy. The real danger is the diversion of tourists, shoppers, and business visitors — people who make substantial contribution to the economy. Hong Kong's prospects depend critically on its role as a business centre. Its roles as a financial centre, a logistics centre, and a shopping paradise are derived from its ease of access from around the world. This edge, which Hong Kong possesses at present, must never be compromised. Hong Kong's challenge is to determine how aviation policies can be shaped to maintain this edge amidst strong competition.

What will be the likely scenario if fifth-freedom access is liberalized? There are two aspects that must be addressed in answering this question. First, consider Hong Kong's position in cross-Pacific traffic. If fifth-freedom traffic is liberalized, more flights will serve the flight markets between Hong Kong and North America, especially the West Coast. Airlines in the Southeast Asia region are well positioned to take advantage of these opportunities. Second and perhaps more important are flight markets within the Asia region. Because of its central location, Hong Kong is but a short distance away from Korea, Japan, and Taiwan in the Northeast, and from Thailand, Malaysia, Singapore, Indonesia, and the Philippines in the South and Southeast. Hong Kong is already the origin and destination of a large portion of intraregional traffic. The continuing growth of China will further boost this traffic. With liberalization, airlines from countries around Hong Kong can use fifth-freedom rights to make convenient connections via Hong Kong.

Notes

1. For a detailed discussion, see Kwong (1988). For a more recent discussion, see the La Croix and Wolff (1996) article included in Pacific Economic Cooperation Council (1996).

2. Cathay Pacific is far larger than Dragonair. Immediately before the 1996 restructuring, Cathay Pacific carried nine times as many passengers as Dragonair did.

CHAPTER 5

The Hotel Industry

Introduction

The hotel industry is one of the most important factors in the development of tourism. Hotels provide not only accommodation for visitors but also dining and entertainment facilities. Hotel cost is one important factor affecting visitors' destination choices. In 1995 visitors to Hong Kong spent about 30% of the money they expended during their stay on hotel bills. Besides having maintain reasonably priced hotels, Hong Kong should maintain high-quality service. The reason is that visitors are generally well-travelled people and they naturally compare the service quality in Hong Kong with that of other cities. Both pricing of hotels and quality of service are important components in the development of tourism.

While the importance of good and affordable hotels is indisputable, the evolution of the economy of Hong Kong is putting increasing stress on the industry. High land prices and rising wages are pushing up the costs of hotel operation. The result is that some hotel owners have found it profitable to convert hotels into office buildings. The supply of hotel rooms in Hong Kong has declined slightly in recent years, despite a rising number of visitors. Demand and supply factors combined to push up room rates which are among the highest in Asia. Hong Kong is one of the fifteen cities in the world with the highest-priced hotel rooms. In terms of accommodation, Hong Kong is indeed an expensive destination. To maintain its flow of visitors, Hong Kong has to offer a great deal — business opportunities, shopping facilities, excellent dining,

Table 5.1

Hotel Statistics, 1986–95

Year*	No. of Hotels	Growth (%)	No. of Rooms	Growth (%)	No. of Employees	Growth (%)	Occupancy (%)	Staff per room
1986	57		20,230		24,038		85	1.19
1987	56	–1.8	21,022	3.9	25,684	7	90	1.22
1988	65	16.1	22,882	8.8	29,191	14	92	1.28
1989	69	6.2	27,031	18.1	32,629	12	79	1.21
1990	75	8.7	28,146	4.1	33,829	4	79	1.20
1991	82	9.3	31,163	10.7	36,077	7	75	1.16
1992	86	4.9	33,534	7.6	36,769	2	82	1.10
1993	88	2.3	34,044	1.7	36,921	0	87	1.08
1994	85	–3.4	33,490	–1.6	36,436	–1	85	1.09
1995	86	1.2	33,052	–1.3	34,852	–4	85	1.05

Source: *A Statistical Review of Tourism 1995*, HKTA.

Note: * All columns except "Occupancy" refer to year-end figures.

high-quality entertainment — in order to compensate for the high rates.

Another threat to the industry is manpower shortage. Rising wages are a problem, but that is only the tip of the iceberg. Hotels find it increasingly difficult to hire the right people. Young people from increasingly affluent families are generally unwilling to embark on a career in hotels. The turnover rate is rather high. The manpower problems have made it hard to maintain service quality. The hotel industry will face greater challenge than before in keeping the personal touch that is so valuable in a hospitality business. Relative to other developing countries in the region, Hong Kong is at a distinct disadvantage in this regard.

General Picture

The hotel industry consists of a wide range of hotels and hostels of differing qualities. At the end of 1995 there were 86 hotels, hostels, and boarding-houses in Hong Kong that were registered members of the Hong Kong Tourist Association (HKTA). There were undoubtedly more establishments in town. The registered ones provided more than 33,000 rooms in 1995 and employed some 35,000 workers. There was roughly one employee to every room. During the last decade, the occupancy rate was uniformly high. It has never dropped below 75%.

Table 5.1 presents the general picture of the hotel industry during the period from 1986 to 1995. The number of registered hotels, hostels, and boarding-houses grew from 57 in 1986 to 86 in 1995. The number of rooms grew from about 20,000 to 33,000. Hotels did not increase much in size. The average hotel had around 350 to 380 rooms. Hotel capacity did not grow particularly fast. From the table, we can also see that most of the growth occurred before 1992. After 1992 there was little growth in hotel capacity. There were actually fewer rooms available at the end of 1995 than there were in 1992.

Occupancy was rather high throughout the period. The most crowded years were 1987 and 1988, when occupancy rates reached

90 and 92%, respectively. These percentages were averages over the entire year. There were months, such as March and October, when demand was consistently higher. When occupancy rates reached an annual average of 90% or higher, hotels were practically packed in the peak months. The quietest years were 1989, 1990, and 1991. In 1991 in particular, occupancy dropped to 75%, as a number of new hotels went into business. After 1991 occupancy climbed to over 80% and remained there until 1995.

Singapore's situation provides some interesting comparisons, as given in the *Yearbook of Statistics Singapore*. In 1995 Singapore received around 7 million visitors, against Hong Kong's 10 million. The average length of stay in Singapore was 3.4 days, against Hong Kong's 3.9 days — not a significant difference. Singapore had 27,471 rooms, and Hong Kong had 33,052 rooms. Occupancy rates were roughly the same, at around 85% in both places. If one puts these numbers together, around one in three visitor days spent in Singapore were accommodated by registered hotels, while the corresponding number in Hong Kong was around one in four. One reason for the difference is that many visitors in Hong Kong came from China and did not need hotel accommodation, or they were accommodated in lodgings not registered with the HKTA. Regardless of the reason, hotel rates did reflect the difference, for hotels in Hong Kong were 37% more expensive than were those in Singapore. If Hong Kong wants to reduce hotel rates to the level of Singapore's, approximately 10,000 more rooms, or 26 new hotels of average size, would be needed. This is clearly impossible given the tight land supply.

In Hong Kong, the staff-to-room ratio did not show any improvement in the period from 1986 to 1995. This is worrisome. In the hotel business, service quality is a top priority. To maintain service quality, manpower is the single most important factor. Machinery, equipment, and modern technology cannot replace people to any significant extent. A declining staff-to-room ratio is a real warning signal of quality deterioration. As is shown in Table 5.1, in 1986, when there were 20,000 rooms in the industry, 24,000 employees were hired, for a staff-to-room ratio of 1.2. This ratio improved slightly in the following two years, as hotels went into a boom in terms of occupancy, but it started to decline after 1988. As of 1995, the staff-to-room ratio had fallen to about 1. The industry staff-to-room ratio norm is 0.97 for a high-tariff hotel. The industry-wide average of Hong Kong hotels is now dropping very close to this benchmark.[1]

Are Rates Too High?

The hotel industry is not regulated economically by the government. Hotels are free to charge their own rates. Hotel rates are basically determined by market demand and supply, and rates do respond rapidly to market conditions. High hotel rates are an indication of high demand or tight supply or a combination of the two. Regardless of the reason, high hotel rates deter potential visitors. Travellers may choose another destination or cut short their stay. Either way, Hong Kong will receive less income by way of tourism, which will have a negative impact on the economy. Nevertheless, high hotel rates have not necessary made hotel operators lose money. Hotels, in particular, stand to gain from the high rates, as room revenue increases in the absence of any increase in costs. A further advantage is that visitors who can afford high rates will probably spend more on food and beverages as well, which gives rise to additional revenue.

One factor that affects the supply of hotels is the price of land. The government leases land for the construction of hotels to land developers. Developers may choose to construct hotels or office buildings on land leased for commercial use. Existing hotels can also be demolished for redevelopment into office buildings. If the price of office space increases, developers will have a stronger incentive to build more office buildings and fewer hotels. In 1995 two luxury hotels were redeveloped into office buildings. The theory is that when the rental rates for office space increase, fewer hotel rooms will be available on the market, and so room rates increase. This is a pure supply-side story that has nothing to do with visitor arrival numbers.

Chapter 5

Table 5.2
Room Rate Comparison among Major Asian Cities

	Average room rate (US$)	Revenue per available room (US$)	Occupancy (%)
Tokyo	176	136.0	77
Seoul	157	124.5	80
Hong Kong	**148**	**129.5**	**87**
Taipei	130	102.8	79
Sydney	126	97.7	78
Shanghai	111	75.1	68
Jakarta	110	73.2	67
Singapore	109	87.3	80
Manila	102	70.3	69
Beijing	94	71.2	76
Bali	85	62.3	73
Kuala Lumpur	84	64.2	77
Bangkok	67	47.2	70
Xian	34	17.6	52

Source: *Trends in the Hotel Industry, Asia Pacific Region,* PKF Consulting Ltd.
Note: Statistics are for year ended August 1996.

How high are the room rates in Hong Kong?. Table 5.2 shows the rates in some of the major Asian cities for the year ending in August 1996. Topping the list was Tokyo, with an average room rate of US$176. Second was Seoul, with an average rate of US$156; Hong Kong was third at US$148. Although there was a margin of US$20 between Tokyo and Hong Kong, the margin depended very much on the exchange rate of the yen versus the U.S. dollar. As the yen has weakened recently, the margin would have diminished a great deal. The margin between Seoul and Hong Kong was rather insignificant. Hong Kong hotels were indeed one of the most expensive ones in Asia, significantly more expensive than Taipei, Sydney, Shanghai, Jakarta, Singapore, and Manila. Hong Kong was 50% more expensive than Beijing, Bali, Kuala Lumpur, Bangkok, and Xian. Room rates in Bangkok averaged only US$67 and those in Xian averaged only US$34.

Despite the high room rates, hotels in Hong Kong have very high occupancy.[2] Table 5.2 shows that in the year ending in

Table 5.3
Average Room Rate Comparison among Major Cities in the World, 1990–94

	1990	1991	1992	1993	1994
Shanghai	not avail.	A	A	A	B
Frankfurt	B	C	C	B	B
Hong Kong	**B**	**A**	**A**	**B**	**B**
Berlin	C	D	D	C	B
Milan	E	E	D	C	B
Warsaw	C	C	D	C	B
Taipei	C	B	C	C	C
Seoul	B	B	B	B	C
Rome	E	D	D	C	C
New York	C	C	C	C	C
London	E	E	E	C	C
Zurich	E	D	D	D	D
Geneva	E	E	F	E	F
Tokyo	D	E	F	H	F
Paris	F	F	G	G	G

Source: *Growth in Average Room Rates*, PKF Consulting Ltd.
Note: The fifteen cities were the ones that had the highest room rates in 1994
          worldwide.
Categories: A = below US$100   B = US$100–US$125
             C = US$125–US$150   D = US$150–US$175
             E = US$175–US$200   F = US$200–US$225
             G = US$225–US$250   H = above US$250

August 1996 Hong Kong, had the highest occupancy rate in Asia, at 87%. The high occupancy allowed hotels to generate high revenue on a per-room basis. Per-room revenue in Hong Kong was second only to that of Tokyo. Table 5.2 shows that, across Asian cities, the room rate correlates with the occupancy. Hotels did not adjust room rates quickly enough in response to market conditions. If this theory is correct, Hong Kong hotel rates have the potential to increase much more.

Hong Kong was among the 15 cities in the world with the highest room rates. Available data for this comparison are a bit dated and imprecise. Nevertheless, the overall picture confirming this comparison may be seen in Table 5.3. In 1994 the 15 cities were, in order of increasing room rates, Shanghai, Frankfurt, Hong Kong, Berlin, Milan, Warsaw, Taipei, Seoul, Rome, New York, London, Zurich, Geneva, Tokyo, and Paris. Most of these cities are financial centres. Not all financial centres are equally expensive, however. Singapore, for example, while being a financial centre is not among the top 15 most expensive cities in terms of room rates. It is still competitive when it comes to hotel accommodation.

In Table 5.3, rates are classified into eight categories, from A (the lowest, below US$100) to H (the highest, above US$250). Hong Kong rates fell in category B in 1990, went down to category A in 1991 (as occupancy decreased), remained in category A in 1992, went up to category B in 1993, and stayed there in 1994. They would have moved into category C in 1995, according to Table 5.2. It is likely that rates would have reached category D in 1996, and, because of the boom caused by the 1997-handover, would have reached category E or higher in 1997.

Until the completion of new hotels associated with the Chek Lap Kok airport and at sites along the airport railway occurs, room rates in Hong Kong will remain high. As a result, Hong Kong will become less attractive as a holiday destination. Only business travellers will be able to afford Hong Kong. To the hotel industry, Hong Kong will become a high-revenue sector on a global scale. Hotels will be able to afford to engage in frequent refurbishment and to invest in employee training.

Making Money?

The hotel industry has been rather profitable in recent years. Table 5.4 presents data in support of this claim. In the period from 1993 to 1995 operating profits for the industry increased rapidly. Income before taxes almost doubled, from HK$2.7 billion in 1993 to HK$5.3 billion in 1995. The increase was brought about mainly by the increase in room rates. The average room rate increased 43%, from HK$764 in 1993 to HK$1,093 in 1995. During this period, hotel profits increased much faster than did room rates, the reason

Table 5.4
Hotel Financial Statistics, 1993–95

	1993	1994	1995
Revenue			
Rooms (HK$ million)	7,586	9,548	10,418
Food & beverage (HK$ million)	5,661	5,463	5,973
Others (HK$ million)	1,138	1,894	2,010
Total revenue (HK$ million)	14,385	16,905	18,401
Expenses (HK$ million)	11,614	12,582	13,105
Income before tax (HK$ million)	2,771	4,323	5,296
No. of rooms available	31,275	31,256	30,813
IBT per room (HK$)	88,607	138,311	171,874
IBT over revenue (%)	19.3	25.6	28.8
Average room rate (HK$)	764	986	1,093
Occupancy (%)	87	85	85

Source: *Hong Kong Hotel Industry,* 1995, 1996, Hong Kong Hotels Association.
Note: Sample comprises High Tariff A and B Hotels and Medium-Tariff Hotels.
          IBT stands for income before tax.

being that the cost of operation remained rather stable. What has been frequently observed in the industry is that given a stable cost environment, profits fluctuate much more than do room rates. Since room rates change according to market conditions, the outcome is that hotel operation profits depend very much on external conditions. The rapid increases in room rates during this period were caused partly by increasing visitor arrivals and partly by the decrease in room supply due to the closure of two major hotels for redevelopment.

Another interesting observation illustrated by Table 5.4 is that food and beverage revenue accounts for a large proportion of total revenue. When room rates were low, as they were in 1993, food and beverage became relatively more important. Much of the food and beverage revenue came from local customers. Food and beverage

Table 5.5
Revenue and Cost Structure of the Hotel Industry
(%)

Revenue Item	1993	1994	1995
Room sales	52.7	56.5	56.6
Food sales	27.7	25.6	25.9
Beverage sales	7.5	6.8	6.5
Minor-operated departments	4.0	3.9	3.5
Telephone sales	4.0	3.8	3.3
Rental and other incomes	2.8	2.4	2.7
Other food and beverage sales	1.4	1.2	1.4
Total	100.0	100.0	100.0

Cost Item	1993	1994	1995
Payroll and related expenses	36.6	36.3	38.5
Departmental expenses	13.0	13.7	12.8
Food cost	11.3	11.0	11.7
Rent	10.0	7.7	6.0
Management fee	4.3	5.0	5.3
Depreciation and amortization	4.6	4.7	4.1
Energy costs	4.7	4.6	4.5
Interest	2.4	4.2	4.1
Administrative & general	3.5	3.4	3.4
Marketing	3.2	3.4	3.1
Property operation and maintenance	2.5	2.7	2.5
Other fixed charges	2.2	1.7	2.2
Beverage cost	1.7	1.7	1.8
Total	100.0	100.0	100.0

Source: *Hong Kong Hotel Industry 1995, 1996,* Hong Kong Hotels Association; HKTA; Horwath Asia Pacific.

Note: Percentage totals may not add up to 100 due to rounding.

represent a steady source of revenue in an otherwise volatile business.

For a more thorough understanding of the hotel business, we take a look at revenue and cost structures. As is shown in Table 5.5, room sales accounted for more than half of total revenue in the period from 1993 to 1995. In 1993 room sales accounted for 53% of total revenue. This figure rose to 57% in 1994 and 1995. Room sales are relatively more important when room rates are higher. On the other hand, room sales, together with food and beverage sales, accounted for almost 90% of total revenue from 1993 to 1995. Other revenue sources, such as telephone charges, rental income from the shopping arcade, laundry services, and so on are relatively insignificant.

On the cost side, the bulk of costs are accounted for by payroll and related expenses. In 1993 this cost item accounted for 36% of total costs. The figure rose to 39% in 1995. The impact of wage rates on profitability is rather significant. At 39% of total cost, a 10% increase in wage rates would lead to a 4% increase in total cost. This cost increase would cut into the operating margin. Taking the profit margin as 28%, for example, the 10% increase in wages would reduce the profit margin to 25%, cutting profit by some 11%. The operating profit of the hotel business is therefore rather sensitive to the level of wages.

Besides payroll, other cost items, such as departmental expenses, food costs, rent, management fees, depreciation, energy costs, interest, administration, marketing, property operation, maintenance, and beverage costs are, as individual items, not very significant. Increases in one or two of these cost items are unlikely to seriously affect profit.

One cost that is not reflected in financial statements is the income that could have been generated from redeveloping the hotel building into an office building. The profit margin of 26% for the industry as a whole in 1994 might have been perceived by hotel owners as being too low when compared to that of office building development. Most hotel owners are land developers; two major hotels, the Hilton and the Victoria, were redeveloped in 1995.

Hotel Shortage?

From the point of view of tourism development, hotels constitute an infrastructure. More vacancies in hotels bring down room rates and it would also make arranging a Hong Kong trip easier. To hotel owners, however, more hotels mean stiffer competition and lower

Table 5.6

Number of Hotel Rooms and Occupancy, 1981–95

	High-Tariff Hotels		Medium-Tariff Hotels		Hostels / Guest Houses		Total	
	Rooms	Occupancy (%)	Rooms	Occupancy (%)	Rooms	Occupancy (%)	Rooms	Occupancy (%)
1981	13,837	88	1,753	85	733	86	16,323	87
1982	14,935	83	1,796	81	684	82	17,415	82
1983	14,999	83	1,752	79	819	86	17,570	83
1984	15,377	89	1,785	84	869	87	18,031	89
1985	15,311	88	1,680	90	1,189	85	18,180	88
1986	16,762	87	2,060	80	1,408	73	20,230	85
1987	16,970	90	3,035	89	1,017	86	21,022	90
1988	18,542	91	3,430	93	910	91	22,882	92
1989	22,157	80	3,949	77	925	86	27,031	79
1990	22,565	79	4,531	76	1,050	86	28,146	79
1991	23,451	76	6,535	75	1,177	74	31,163	75
1992	23,049	83	9,128	82	1,357	82	33,534	82
1993	23,413	86	9,294	89	1,337	88	34,044	87
1994	23,104	85	9,062	85	1,324	87	33,490	85
1995	22,226	85	9,167	84	1,659	86	33,052	85

Source: *Annual Digest of Statistics*, Census and Statistics Department; *A Statistical Review of Tourism*, HKTA.

profits. To them, occupancy rates rarely reach 100%, and they have never seen queues forming outside hotels. They cannot see any hotel shortage.

Deciding on the right volume of hotel supply is a conundrum. There are, broadly speaking, three categories of hotels: high-tariff hotels, medium-tariff hotels, and hostels or boarding-houses. These hotels differ not only in room rates, but also in staff-to-room ratio and the availability of amenities such as swimming pools, business centres and room service. In Hong Kong, most hotels fall into the high-tariff category, although more medium-tariff hotels and hostels have been built in recent years. In 1981, 85% of all hotels were high-tariff hotels. In 1995, 67%, still a dominating proportion, were high-tariff hotels. Over the period, medium-tariff hotels were the fastest-growing category, despite a small initial base. This trend reflects the growing importance in recent years of short-haul source markets such as the People's Republic of China, Taiwan, and South East Asia.

Table 5.6 shows the composition of the hotel population from 1981 to 1995. We first comment on some long-term changes. In 1981 there were in total 16,323 hotel rooms. In 1995 there were 33,052 rooms, representing a growth rate of 102%. In the same period, the number of visitor arrivals grew from 2.5 million to almost 8 million, both figures excluding the arrivals from the People's Republic of China, as these visitors could usually find accommodation outside hotels. The growth rate in arrivals was therefore 215%, a much higher percentage than that of the increase in hotel supply. Yet occupancy in 1981 stood at 87%, while in 1995 it stood at 85%. The length of stay per visitor (not shown) did not change dramatically in this period.

It is somewhat puzzling that hotels in Hong Kong have been able to service more visitors in recent years. There are two conjectures explaining this phenomenon. One is that, in recent years, more visitors travelled in families that could share rooms. The other is that a number of the "visitors" were actually Hong Kong residents who had emigrated abroad in previous years. When they returned for a short stay, they did not need hotel accommodation.

Regardless of the reason, it is clear that the statistics shown in Table 5.6 cannot be used as the sole basis for the determination of the appropriate level of hotel supply.

Hotel developers are also concerned about short-term shocks that are difficult to anticipate. Hotel profits in Hong Kong depend largely on room rates which are easily affected by market conditions. Table 5.6 gives some indication of the impact of such shocks. The period from 1981 to 1995 can be roughly divided into three periods — a few years of slow growth in hotel supply, followed by a few years of fast growth, followed by almost complete stagnation. The period from 1981 to 1988 saw slow growth in hotel supply. In eight years' time, the number of hotel rooms grew from 16,323 to 22,882, about a 40% increase. If one looks deeper into the individual categories, one finds that the number of medium-tariff hotels increased rather rapidly between 1986 and 1988, but because of their small base the growth was not noticeable at the industry level. The slow growth in supply did create some tightness, as the occupancy rate climbed steadily from 87% in 1981, to 82% in 1982, to 92% in 1988. The supply tightness prompted the building of more hotels. The lead time was long, however. The planning, design, and construction phases took three to four years. By the time the new hotels hit the market, conditions had changed. The 4 June 1989 incident in Beijing and the Gulf War in 1990 and 1991 sent the tourism industry into a recession. Meanwhile, new hotels were being completed, rapidly expanding hotel capacity. From 1988 to 1992 the number of hotel rooms grew 32%, from 22,882 rooms to 33,534 rooms. As a result of growing supply and shrinking demand, occupancy dropped to 75% in 1991. Excess capacity slowed the building of new hotels and set off another few years of slow expansion in supply. Coupled with the redevelopment of two major hotels, the supply from 1993 to 1995 actually went down. While there were 34,044 rooms in 1993, there were only 33,052 rooms in 1995. At the moment, although formal figures are not available, the industry appears to be set for another period of "shortage", as visitor arrivals are expected to set new records in 1996 and 1997, while no major expansion took place in 1996.

The hotel industry clearly follows a distinct cyclical pattern. This is not a unique feature of Hong Kong hotels. The same type of pattern has been observed in Singapore. When the government plans the hotel industry in the future, both long-term demand and short-term fluctuations should be taken into consideration. The government should refrain from granting hotel construction permits quickly on the strength of temporary upswings.

Land Use

All the land in Hong Kong is ultimately owned by the government. So-called "landlords" are holders of land leases with specified tenure from the government. The development of land is strictly controlled by the government; the type of use to which a piece of land can be put is specified in the lease. There are three major categories of use: residential, industrial, and commercial. Hotels are classified as commercial and are in the same category as are office buildings. Redevelopment of built-up sites requires the approval of the government. The government does not normally approve redevelopment into a building that belongs to a different category. A hotel can be redeveloped into an office building with the approval of the government, but a residential site or an industrial site cannot be redeveloped for the construction of a hotel. According to past experience, as the real estate market has been rather volatile, there have been cases in which half-built hotels were converted into office blocks, where newly completed hotels were not opened for business, pending decision to be converted, and where well-managed hotels were demolished for redevelopment.

Another factor that affects hotel capacity has to do with the "plot ratio" imposed by the government. For fire safety reasons, and because of environmental effects on the surrounding area, the government lays down stringent rules governing the proportion of a site that can be built up. The plot ratio differs according to the type of building and its location. In the past, the plot ratio for hotels allowed a smaller useable floor space than that for office buildings. This practice created an extra incentive for land developers to develop office buildings. In recent years, the government has been making concessions to put the plot ratio for hotels on par with that of office buildings. This practice encouraged the building of more hotels and was welcomed by the tourism business.

Another recent change in government policy is that it has practically created a fourth land-use category, that of hotels. As trials, two sites have been zoned specifically for the building of hotels. Creating a hotel-use category would ensure a stable stock of hotel rooms, reducing short-term spikes in room rates that are caused by supply shrinkage. The government hopes to put into existence a hotel land market. There are clear gains and losses associated with this policy change. On the positive side, there will be no conversion of hotels into office buildings. The supply of hotel rooms will be more stable. As has been the case in Singapore, sites have been zoned specifically for hotels. In the late 1980s, when there was a large excess of hotel rooms in Singapore, even luxury hotels had to cut room rates down to US$30 to US$40 to keep their operations running. Low room rates supported the tourism industry when external conditions were not favourable. On the negative side, restricting the use of a site to hotels exclusively inhibits the adjustment of the economy to market changes. A site zoned for hotels may sometimes be put to more valuable use if it is redeveloped for office use. Adding restrictions to a land lease also reduces its market value. The government will not then be able to maximize the revenue from sales of land. The amount of land that ought to be zoned exclusively for hotel development requires, therefore, the striking of a delicate balance between the gains that accrue from the development of the tourism industry and the losses that arise from the reduction in land value.

Manpower Difficulties

The most critical factor in the successful operation of a hotel is probably the quantity and quality of manpower. This is particularly true in the case of high-tariff hotels. Most high-tariff hotels in Hong Kong are owned by land developers and managed by multinationals. Only multinationals have the expertise and the networks necessary to run these hotels successfully. The profit of hotel operation depends very much on the level of wages. The major difficulties most hotel operators face are related to manpower. These difficulties are high wage levels, declining quality of personnel, and fast turnover.

Hotel jobs are very demanding. First, life in a hotel is rather regimented. Workers are expected to take orders from superiors without hesitation. Workers have to be absolutely punctual, loyal, neat, and disciplined. They do not have an office or a desk of their own. Unlike the majority of the working population, they are not allowed to carry pagers or mobile phones to work. Second, most hotel workers have to work shifts, and they usually do not have a choice about which shifts to work. Many people cannot cope with alternating day and night shifts. Moreover, hotel work is demanding. Hotel workers rarely have a chance to sit down and take a break. Third, senior positions are usually promoted from below. Even executives are usually long-time veterans of the floor. They are rarely business school graduates. In short, a hotel career is a tough one that is suitable only for the young. Opportunities for middle-aged workers are rather limited.

Because hotel jobs are demanding, it is difficult to find qualified workers at low-wage rates. This is particularly true in the case in Hong Kong and other international cities where the market wage is generally high. Despite advances in science and technology, the quality of hotel service is still highly dependent on manpower. Hospitality is very much a human touch. According to interviews with hotel managers, at least in Hong Kong, machines cannot take the place of workers, and the demand for good workers has not diminished. It is feared that, as the general educational level improves, fewer young people would be interested in a hotel career.

While the quantity of manpower is important, the quality of manpower is equally critical. It is believed that worker quality, or, more accurately, service quality, in the hotel business is directly linked to the attitude of the worker. In a tight labour market situation, and in the presence of high-paying jobs such as those of sales representatives and real estate agents, hotels find it hard to recruit workers with the right attitude. Of course, these arguments may all boil down to hotels needing to raise their wages and see their profits cut.

A third difficulty that hotels in Hong Kong have to face is worker training. Hotels generally prefer to run their own training programmes, which are largely carried out on the job. Many skills can only be acquired from constant practice. Training is jeopardized if the turnover rate is too high. The turnover rate is particularly high among base-level workers. Many such workers find their jobs too demanding, both physically and emotionally, and they change jobs after a short trial period. Consequently, floor workers are generally inexperienced. The responsibility of their superiors becomes more onerous. The stress on supervisors and middle managers becomes heavier, and thus the turnover problem filters upwards in the hierarchy.

The government has done a great deal towards providing trained hotel workers. It has been running regular hotel courses under the Vocational Training Council. The Hong Kong Polytechnic University has been running an honours degree programme in hotel and catering management. There is even an examination subject called Travel and Tourism at the Certificate of Education (Form 5) level. But hotels do not find these programmes very helpful. The general feeling is that the programmes are not producing the type of workers that they need. Most of the formally trained students, even if they do join a hotel after graduation, do not stay long. Perhaps this is because they are "over-educated". From the point of view of hotels, academic training is unimportant. The selection and training of hotel workers seem to be best left to the hotels themselves.

The solution to the manpower problem is the continuation of the labour importation scheme. The hotel industry has been the major employer applying for government quotas to import foreign workers, including a sizeable proportion from China. The arrangement has worked out smoothly. Even though hotels have to provide accommodation and a minimum wage, they find the scheme helpful. Some critics of the scheme query the hotels' reluctance to hire workers released from the shrinking manufacturing sector. The reality is that the released manufacturing workers cannot easily fit the requirements of hotel work. They may be trainable for some behind-the-scenes jobs such as cleaning and housekeeping, but opportunities there are not abundant. Most of these released workers are middle-aged. Although the government has provided retraining programmes for them, few end up working in hotels.

Summing Up

In the coming years, Hong Kong will continue to be a high-cost destination as far as hotel accommodation is concerned. The tight supply of land and the rapid growth of visitor traffic will sustain hotel rates at a high level. The land use policy of the government should be to ensure a steady, predictable supply of hotels with modest growth capacities. The hotel-use category, introduced recently, is a step in the right direction. To make up for high rates, superior service has to be offered, and in this regard the manpower situation is the foremost problem. The government should work closely with the hotel business in designing retraining programmes. More important perhaps is the continuation of the worker importation scheme, which allows hotels to select and recruit workers of their choice from China and other countries.

Notes

1. According to *Hong Kong Hotel Industry 1996*, the staff to room ratio for High Tariff A hotels in 1995 was 1.38, lower than the industry norm, for hotels of this class, of 1.60. For High Tariff B hotels, the ratio was 1.04, marginally exceeding the industry norm for this class of 0.97.

2. As hotel rates are not government regulated, their level is determined purely by market conditions, i.e. demand and supply conditions.

CHAPTER 6

A Shopping Paradise

Introduction

Shopping accounts for about half of all visitor spending in Hong Kong. In 1995 visitors spent 37 billion dollars on shopping. They bought a wide variety of consumer goods. Most of those goods sold in 1995 were not produced in Hong Kong or by Hong Kong people. Hong Kong merely acted as an intermediary in producing and sourcing goods from all over the world, and as a retailer by displaying the goods in shops waiting for customers to purchase them. Hong Kong is probably unique in its ability to create such a large retail industry.[1]

Hong Kong thrives on selling style goods — clothing, shoes, handbags, jewellery, watches, cosmetics and so on. People buy style goods to make a conspicuous statement to signify their taste and sophisticated lifestyle. Because Hong Kong residents are exposed to world trends, retailers are well positioned to gauge from the globe-trotting locals what style goods visitors would want for boosting self-image.[2] One advantage of retailing is its modest requirements in terms of set-up costs and formal education. It is also highly flexible. If a certain line does not sell well, a different line could be sold next season. No major retooling or change in machinery would be required.[3]

That Hong Kong is losing its advantage as a shopping paradise has long been a concern to the government and industry. The source of this concern is that rising local costs are forcing retailers to charge higher prices. As most goods sold in Hong Kong are not locally produced, visitors can buy the same goods in other cities, probably at lower prices. If Hong Kong loses its attraction as a shopping mecca, tourism will suffer considerably. While this is a plausible scenario, the reality appears less grim. Just how competitive is Hong Kong as a shopping centre?

According to surveys of retail prices in the world's major cities, Hong Kong is still the cheapest place to buy a wide variety of goods. It is true, however, that the price gap is closing. Prices in other cities in the region are becoming more competitive as tariffs are cut and wholesalers build up a wider distribution network to cover those cities.

Another approach to assessing the competitiveness of Hong Kong retailing is by analysing the cost structure of the retail industry. People fear that rising wages and rental rates in Hong Kong are eroding its competitive advantages. A quantitative analysis in this chapter shows that, while cost increases have had a negative impact on profits, the retail industry has been able to maintain in recent years gross and net profit margins that compare favourably with the margins of a decade ago.

The retail industry is not in imminent danger of declining. The key to its future success is in keeping the volume of business high. A high business volume will spread the overhead cost out and sustain the net profit margin. So long as inventory turns over quickly, retailers will be able to stock the latest models in their product lines. At the industry level, a high business volume will attract more retailers to enter the tourist market; and more retailers in competition with one another will help expanding the range of goods offered in Hong Kong.

Shopping Favourites

A major feature about tourism in Hong Kong is that visitors buy large quantities of style goods. When buying style goods, customers typically want to take a close look at them, feel them in their hands, and perhaps compare different brands and models. The variety of goods and their concentration in one area are essential in the retailing of style goods. Hong Kong's strength in respect of satisfying the needs of time-pressed tourists lies precisely in the great variety of goods that visitors can find in a district, and in the clustering of many shops. Visitors need not spend much time comparing merchandise and prices. Shops situated side by side derive mutual benefits from one another. They attract more customers by virtue of a collective prominence and they offer complementary goods. The customer may choose a shirt from one store, find a suit next door, and buy a pair of matching shoes across the street. Within the category of style goods, there is hardly any brand or any model that a tourist cannot find in Hong Kong. One-stop shopping is therefore one of the strongest advantages that Hong Kong possesses.

One may want to take a closer look at what exactly visitors are buying in Hong Kong. Table 6.1 provides an indication. In the table, there are 22 broadly defined items. We also identify seven source markets for visitors — Japan, Taiwan, China, the United States, the United Kingdom, Germany and Australia. Visitors from different source markets generally show different buying preferences. For each market, the first column shows the expenditure on each item in 1995 and the second column shows the percentage share of each item. Items that accounted for 1% or less of spending by each source market are not shown separately, but are grouped under "others". The specific items identified in the table accounted for 94% or more of the spending from each source market in 1995. Practically all visitors' shopping interests are thus captured in Table 6.1. Highlights of shopping patterns are presented below, featuring tailored clothing, ready-to-wear clothing, jewellery and foodstuff.

Tailored clothing (first row of Table 6.1) was a popular item in 1995, especially among visitors from the West — the United States, the United Kingdom and Germany. More than 17% of the spending by American tourists and more than 13% of that by the British were on tailored clothing. Hong Kong's advantage here has always been quick delivery, good craftsmanship, a wide range of materials to choose from, and reasonable prices relative to those of a visitor's home country. The price difference factor is evidently an important

Table 6.1
Shopping Preferences by Shopping Items and Source Market, 1995

Shopping Items	Taiwan HK$ million	%	P.R.C. HK$ million	%	Japan HK$ million	%	USA HK$ million	%	Australia HK$ million	%	Germany HK$ million	%	UK HK$ million	%
Tailored clothing	65.6	0.7	13.5	0.2	90.4	1.2	226.0	17.3	29.4	4.4	35.7	7.0	60.7	13.5
Ready-to-wear clothing	4,248.6	45.5	3,090.7	36.9	1,150.7	15.2	309.5	23.7	179.9	27.0	108.5	21.2	113.3	25.1
Fabric	3.6	0.0	2.9	0.0	31.9	0.4	9.7	0.7	9.3	1.4	2.8	0.6	8.0	1.8
Luggage	27.8	0.3	17.7	0.2	219.0	2.9	12.3	0.9	9.1	1.4	5.4	1.1	5.4	1.2
Shoes	423.9	4.5	421.5	5.0	305.9	4.0	27.6	2.1	35.7	5.4	9.9	1.9	4.8	1.1
Handbags	487.0	5.2	192.1	2.3	2,204.0	29.1	17.6	1.4	15.6	2.3	14.1	2.7	8.7	1.9
Photo equipment	248.0	2.7	217.0	2.6	0.0	0.0	50.4	3.9	20.3	3.1	72.6	14.2	40.6	9.0
Spectacles	54.1	0.6	16.9	0.2	24.1	0.3	53.8	4.1	15.0	2.3	16.4	3.2	20.6	4.6
Audio equipment	225.2	2.4	105.5	1.2	36.6	0.5	12.4	1.0	36.5	5.5	17.2	3.4	14.0	3.1
Gold jewellery	368.0	3.9	2,875.6	34.3	358.6	4.7	77.6	6.0	78.6	11.8	58.1	11.3	28.3	6.3
Precious stones	919.9	9.9	192.5	2.3	366.5	4.8	147.5	11.3	36.5	5.5	39.1	7.6	26.3	5.8
Pearls	33.8	0.4	48.1	0.6	15.8	0.2	55.9	4.3	3.4	0.5	17.8	3.5	5.7	1.3
Toys	83.4	0.9	39.7	0.5	15.1	0.2	6.8	0.5	12.7	1.9	4.0	0.8	3.9	0.9
Computers	52.5	0.6	13.6	0.2	15.8	0.2	3.2	0.2	34.6	5.2	10.3	2.0	5.2	1.2
Watches	334.3	3.6	377.5	4.5	430.9	5.7	47.2	3.6	17.0	2.5	33.6	6.6	15.5	3.4
Perfume / cosmetics	538.3	5.8	139.9	1.7	716.0	9.4	11.0	0.8	27.7	4.2	7.7	1.5	6.6	1.5
Alcohol / tobacco	305.1	3.3	33.5	0.4	257.5	3.4	7.9	0.6	5.9	0.9	2.4	0.5	3.0	0.7
Furniture	91.1	1.0	5.9	0.1	0.0	0.0	3.4	0.3	0.7	0.1	0.1	0.0	12.2	2.7
Foodstuffs	117.4	1.3	239.6	2.9	280.1	3.7	5.9	0.5	2.3	0.4	1.1	0.2	3.1	0.7
Souvenirs	72.8	0.8	55.4	0.7	479.4	6.3	123.2	9.4	21.7	3.3	23.3	4.5	31.9	7.1
Antiques / china	210.4	2.3	1.3	0.0	302.9	4.0	11.5	0.9	47.0	7.1	5.5	1.1	14.7	3.3
Medicine / herbs	200.0	2.1	111.6	1.3	110.4	1.5	7.8	0.6	1.8	0.3	0.7	0.1	0.3	0.1
Others	221.3	2.4	174.4	2.2	169.4	2.2	77.4	5.9	26.0	3.9	26.9	5.3	18.2	4.1
Total	9,332.2	100.0	8,386.4	100.0	7,580.9	100.0	1,305.3	100.0	666.4	100.0	512.9	100.0	450.8	100.0

Source: HKTA.

one, for purchases of tailored clothing was not significant among visitors from Japan, Taiwan and China.

Ready-to-wear clothing (second row of Table 6.1) was a different story altogether. Almost half of the total shopping spending of Taiwanese visitors was on ready-to-wear clothing. Equally sizeable was the amount of ready-to-wear clothing bought by visitors from the People's Republic of China, who spent more than one-third of their shopping money on such merchandise. Taiwanese visitors spent HK$4.2 billion, and People's Republic of China visitors spent HK$3.1 billion on ready-to-wear clothing alone. In other markets, ready-to-wear clothing was equally important, accounting for close to one-fourth of the money expended on shopping by visitors from the United States, the United Kingdom, Germany and Australia. It also accounted for 15% of Japanese shopping spending. Although not dominant in share terms, the Japanese did spend HK$1.15 billion on ready-to-wear clothing. Hong Kong was, and still is, the clothing capital of the world. It offers a complete range of clothing — from the very expensive to the very cheap, for every purpose, for every age and for every climate. Ready-to-wear clothing was the largest shopping item for visitors from all markets except those from Japan.

Japanese visitors spend more on handbags than on any other single retail item in 1995. They spent HK$22 billion on handbags alone. This huge amount rendered the spending on handbags by other visitors look very insignificant. The handbags that Japanese visitors purchased were mostly high-end models. These models are much more expensive in Japan than in Hong Kong because of higher import tariffs and distribution costs. Japanese tourists also in Europe where fashionable handbags are made. Although prices in Europe are often lower, Hong Kong has an advantage in being close to Japan and in being able to maintain an adequate stock throughout the year. Many if not most sales representatives of high-end fashion shops in Hong Kong speak Japanese. This capability also helps boost service quality from the perspective of Japanese tourists.

While the Japanese spent large amounts on handbags in 1995, they spent next to nothing on photo equipment, spectacles, audio equipment, pearls, toys, computers and furniture. These items are in most cases cheaper and more sophisticated in Japan than in Hong Kong. Other visitors might not have such "home-made" opportunities in their home countries. The Germans found photo equipment in Hong Kong to be a good bargain. The Americans and the British liked Hong Kong spectacles. The Australians were interested in the audio equipment found in Hong Kong. The Americans and the Germans liked pearls, the Australians liked toys, the Germans and Australians liked computers, and the British liked furniture. The customer base of Hong Kong retailing has been evidently quite broad.

Emerging quickly in importance in recent years has been the jewellery industry. Hong Kong has a well-established industry that makes pure gold ornaments and jewellery. The technology has been in place for a long time. Coupled with the gold industry have been the electroplating industry and a large number of jewellery designers. Building on a solid knowledge foundation, Hong Kong has been able to produce a wide variety of costume jewellery and fine jewellery. The industry received a big boost from the large number of People's Republic of China visitors who bought jewellery both for decoration and as an investment amidst high inflation in China. The shopping pattern of the People's Republic of China visitors is easily observed (column 2, Table 6.1). They spent one-third of their shopping money on ready-to-wear clothing, one-third on jewellery, and one-third on all other retail items.

Also worth mentioning are cosmetics and foodstuffs. Cosmetics were particularly popular among Japanese visitors, who bought more than HK$700 million worth of it in 1995, accounting for close to 10% of their shopping spending. Visitors from Taiwan and the People's Republic of China combined bought roughly the same amount of cosmetics as the Japanese. Almost none of the cosmetics were produced in Hong Kong. As was the case for most ready-to-wear clothing and handbags, cosmetics were all imported. Hong Kong merely acted as an intermediary, a window through which cosmetics from all over the world could be purchased. It is amazing that such an industry could have developed all by itself.[4]

A similar story applies to foodstuffs. That Hong Kong is a culinary capital of the world is well known. It has more than 7,000 restaurants, not including fast-food shops, bars and canteens. Hong Kong also exports a large amount of foodstuffs through tourism. In 1995 visitors from Japan, Taiwan, and the People's Republic of China bought more than HK$600 million worth of foodstuffs. Items purchased were mostly expensive ones such as bird's nest, shark's fin, abalone and other dried seafood. As was the case with cosmetics, none of these items were produced in Hong Kong.

Price Comparison across Cities

Most popular retail items in Hong Kong are imports from all over the world which are then exported through visitors from all over the world. It could be argued that this business is based on a rather fragile foundation. There is no apparent reason for why some other cities in the region could not take Hong Kong's leading position as a distribution intermediary. The argument is even more compelling in view of the rising costs in Hong Kong and other cities' tendency towards reducing their trade barriers.

We attempt to analyze the price competitiveness of Hong Kong retailing from two angles. In the present section we discuss surveys that gauge the price differences of common items sold in Hong Kong and other big cities around the world. In the following section, we then analyze the cost structure of the retail industry and see how seriously the profits of retailers have been affected by rising costs and rental rates. Our analysis shows that Hong Kong has been able to remain competitive. Thanks to the variety of its merchandise and its proximity to source markets, Hong Kong can, still, hope to maintain a competitive edge over other retail markets in the near future.

Comparing prices across cities is not an easy task. In recent years, the HKTA has been commissioning a private consultancy firm to survey prices in eleven large cities, including Hong Kong.

Table 6.2

Retail Price Comparison across Major Cities in the World, 1992–95

	1992	1993	1994	1995
Hong Kong	80	78	71	80
Taipei	87	88	89	82
Singapore	87	81	83	87
London	115	88	89	88
New York	88	106	97	93
Bangkok	103	103	94	99
Paris	112	92	101	101
Sydney	97	104	106	111
Tokyo	114	137	132	113
Frankfurt	109	95	132	118
Toronto	101	128	105	128

Source: *Tourist Price Survey,* Economic Intelligence Unit (1996).

Notes: 1. Cost of a basket of 15 items was calculated for each city.
The average cost over all 15 cities of this basket was set equal to 100.

2. Some goods not available in all cities, in which cases, replacements were used.

3. Sale prices ignored

4. No bargaining over prices

5. Prices included sales taxes and value added tax (VAT).

Table 6.2 shows the results from 1992 to 1995. Besides Hong Kong, the cities covered by the surveys are Taipei, Singapore, London, New York, Bangkok, Paris, Sydney, Tokyo, Frankfurt and Toronto. Thus, the sample consists of the capitals and financial centres of high-income developed countries, as well as the major cities in Asia. The numbers in Table 6.2 are price indexes.

In all four years, Hong Kong appeared to be the cheapest shopping centre in the sample. Taipei and Singapore were also competitive; of the two, Singapore seemed to be getting more expensive. London was also becoming more competitive, partly because of the weak domestic economy and partly because of the weak currency. Slightly less competitive were New York and Bangkok. New York, not unlike other American cities, was actually rather competitive in electronics and American-made goods, although luxury items such as gold watches and high-end handbags tended to be more expensive. In the case of Bangkok, import duties on luxury goods tended to jack up prices, and the small scale of the market tended to reduce the variety of goods available. Other cities, including Paris, Sydney, Tokyo, Frankfurt and Toronto were generally not competitive. Although many luxury style goods are made in France they were actually cheaper in Hong Kong than in Paris. The reason of high taxes in Paris; taxes also made luxury items relatively expensive in Sydney, Frankfurt and Toronto. Tokyo also turned out to be an expensive city. The extent to which it was more expensive that other cities surveyed depended very much on the kind of goods surveyed. While luxury items like handbags and gold watches were expensive in Tokyo, Japanese-made cameras and electronic goods were actually quite competitive. The interpretation of the survey results should be made with care. Small differences in price indexes do not carry much meaning, as the indexes depend heavily on the kind of goods surveyed. Nevertheless, it seems safe to say that the closest competitors to Hong Kong are Taipei and Singapore.

The methodology of the surveys deserves some elaboration. First of all, the surveys identify a number of items that were popular among visitors to Hong Kong. These items were:

two luxury handbags,
a ten-gram 18K gold necklace,
an American brand-name suitcase,
an American brand-name polo shirt,
an American portable computer,
a pair of Swiss-made luxury shoes,
a Swiss-made gold watch,
a Japanese-made discman,
a Japanese audio system,
a Japanese computer game,
a Japanese autofocus camera,
a Japanese video camera,
a pair of French gold-framed spectacles, and
a French luxury perfume.

The items were precisely specified, in most cases with model numbers. In each city, the prices of each item were surveyed. As items could be sold in a variety of outlets, a range of prices for a single item was taken into consideration. The more expensive stores charged higher prices but offered superior service. These prices were then averaged to indicate the typical price of an item in a particular city. Finally, the cost of the entire basket of fifteen items was calculated for each city using the averaged prices. To arrive at the numbers in Table 6.2, the average cost of a basket across all eleven cities was used as a benchmark and was given a price index of 100. Thus the price index of 80 for Hong Kong in 1995 means that the cost of purchasing the basket in Hong Kong was 80% of the worldwide benchmark. Buying the same basket in Toronto at 128 means it would cost 28% more than the worldwide benchmark.

There are a number of difficulties in conducting surveys of this kind. These difficulties tend to affect the reliability of the results. First of all, some items were not available in all cities. When an item could not be found, a close substitute was used as replacement. The price of an available substitute could be considerably higher if it was a newer and more advanced model that had replaced the older and more basic model. Second, prices taken were as a rule regular prices, not sale prices that might remain in effect only for a short period. One could of course argue that sale prices should be taken into account, as visitors will not turn down good bargains. Third, it was assumed that all listed prices were fixed. In the retail sale of some luxury goods bargaining is customary, and even visitors have little difficulty negotiating lower prices. Fourth, prices taken included sales taxes and Value Added Tax (VAT) where applicable. In some countries, goods sold to visitors are not subject to sales tax. Ignoring this provision would bias prices in these cities upwards.

It is difficult to gauge how much methodological complications affect the results shown in Table 6.2. As Taipei and Singapore were the closest competitors, it would be helpful to check to see if they were affected by any of the complications. In the case of Singapore, the audio system and the portable computer were not available and were replaced by more expensive models. Though this adjustment resulted in closing the cost gap between Hong Kong and Singapore by a small margin, it did not have an insignificant impact on the final results. In the case of Taipei, a handbag, the video camera, and the portable computer were not available. Again, the margin was so small that overall results would not have been affected. As for bargaining, sale prices and sales taxes, it is unlikely that these complications would have affected results significantly. Despite the methodological difficulties, the overall conclusion that Hong Kong has been maintaining a price edge over other cities seems to be a robust one.

While Hong Kong might have been the cheapest city surveyed overall, its edge may be a small one. Among items available in Hong Kong, Singapore and Taipei, Hong Kong's prices for the handbags, the shoes, the computer toy and the spectacle frames were the lowest. Singapore had the lowest prices for the suitcase, the perfume, the camera and the necklace. Taipei had the lowest prices for the polo shirt, the discman and the gold watch. Thus, relative to the closest competitors, Hong Kong could boast of offering the lowest prices for only certain items.

An Analysis of Costs

The second approach to assessing the competitiveness of Hong Kong retailing is to estimate the profit margins of retailers. If retailers are making good profits, they are making good returns to their investment, and their businesses will be growing. At the industry level, sufficient profit is an indication that the retail industry is withstanding competitive pressure from other cities. On the other hand, if profits are diminishing, then the industry is in danger of declining. The industry must either move to produce higher-value services or must cut costs by improving operating efficiency. Failure to do either would cause the industry to contract, and investors and workers would move to other industries.

From the financial point of view, the retail business is rather simple. The key personnel are merchandisers and sales representatives. Merchandisers are responsible for buying goods. They have to

Table 6.3

Financial Statistics of the Retail Sector, 1983–92

Financial Item	1983	1984	1985	1986	1987	1988	1989	1990	1991	1992
Sales receipts (HK$ million)	62,089	70,558	73,131	82,910	103,659	127,596	140,587	156,190	187,154	217,229
Gross margin (HK$ million)	13,435	15,672	16,462	19,593	24,805	30,578	35,742	39,489	47,934	55,488
Employee compensation (HK$ million)	3,758	4,351	4,683	5,274	6,199	7,806	9,209	10,128	12,661	14,218
Operating expenses (HK$ million)	6,939	7,712	8,170	9,576	11,909	14,506	17,779	20,627	25,240	28,734
Net profit (HK$ million)	2,738	3,609	3,609	4,743	6,697	8,266	8,754	8,734	10,033	12,536
Gross profit over sales receipts	22%	22%	23%	24%	24%	24%	25%	25%	26%	26%
Net profit over sales receipts	4.41%	5.11%	4.93%	5.72%	6.46%	6.48%	6.23%	5.59%	5.36%	5.77%
Nominal index of retail wages	166.9	196.5	209.8	227.6	259.9	303.6	350.3	393.5	495.5	531.1
Rental index of retail premises	60	55	58	61	69	81	100	112	126	149

Source: *Annual Digest of Statistics*, Census and Statistics Department, Hong Kong.

know customers well and to order the right kind and the right quantity of goods. In some instances goods have to be priced correctly as well, although in most cases retailers markup a fixed percentage. Any buying or pricing mistake would result in the building up of inventory, which ties up working capital and eventually necessitates clearance at discounted prices. Making the correct buying and pricing decisions is only the first half of the story, however. To sell well, the skill and effort of the sales representatives are also very important. In serving source markets in the region, Hong Kong retailers have a distinct advantage in terms of language. Many sales representatives speak Cantonese, Mandarin, and English, and some speak Japanese. Visitors from Japan, Taiwan, China, and Southeast Asia can be readily served.

The first indicator of profitability is gross margin (or gross profit) divided by sales receipts. In the retail business, gross margin is simply the sales revenue minus the cost of goods sold. The gross margin is affected by a number of factors. A clearance sale would reduce the margin, because sales revenue is reduced. Intense competition would tend to reduce prices and therefore reduce the margin. Moving upmarket to sell more exclusive and luxurious items would usually expand the margin, because the markup is usually higher. On the other hand, inventory obsolescence and deterioration, being signs of management failures, would reduce the gross margin. Variations in exchange rates also affect the margin. If the goods are made in Japan and if the Japanese yen appreciates against the Hong Kong dollar, retailers usually have to absorb part of the cost increase, and so the gross margin would be reduced.

Table 6.3 shows the gross margin of the retail industry in Hong Kong during the decade from 1983 to 1992. The retail industry covers all goods retailed in Hong Kong, not just the ones that visitors typically buy. As data that pertain to retailers who exclusively serve the tourism industry are unavailable, the data shown represent the closest picture available. To remove the effect of inflation, we focus on gross margin over sales receipts rather than on gross margin per se. As is shown in the table, gross margin over sales receipts rose steadily throughout the decade, from 22% in 1983 to 26% in 1992. The apparent reason for the increase was a continuous shift towards the retailing of higher-priced goods. In the retailing of high-priced fashion clothing, it is not unusual to apply a markup of 200%; a piece of clothing with a wholesale cost of $100 will retail at $300 in the regular season. Of course, not all goods sell at the full price; some have to be sold at big discounts. So the eventual gross margin would be somewhat smaller. The figures in Table 6.3 pertain to the retailing of all goods, not just fashion clothing. What we learn from the data is that, for the retail industry as a whole, gross profit has historically stood at around 22% to 26%.

It is a well-known fact that wages and rental rates have been rising rapidly in Hong Kong. The important concern is whether the increase in labour and rental costs are eroding the profits of the industry. Net profit after tax, being gross profit minus worker compensation, deductions and taxes, is the bottom line of business operation. Since the tax rate in Hong Kong has not experienced large changes, it can be ignored in the present analysis. The net profit is a measure of the return to the investment made on a retail shop. A rising net profit indicates a growing industry and attracts more investors into the industry. On the other hand, a declining net profit would indicate a shrinking industry as investors move out. Looking at net profit alone is subject to an inflation bias. As prices inflate, the value of the dollar depreciates, and so would the value of the net profit. To remove the effect of inflation, we focus upon the net profit over sales receipts.

Return on investment may be more indicative of profitability, but as data for investment at the industry level are not available, we have to resort to using return on sales as a profitability indicator. As is shown in Table 6.3, net profit over sales receipts rose from 4.4% in 1983 to a peak of 6.5% in 1988 and then declined to 5.8% in 1992. While the profitability of the retail business experienced a downward trend in the second half of the decade, profitability (in absolute terms) was higher at the end of the decade than it was at the beginning. Wages and rental rates did rise rapidly between 1987 and 1992. Between 1983 and 1987, the wage index rose at a rate of about 12% per annum, whereas from 1987 to 1992 it rose at a rate of 15% per annum. For rental rates, the rental index rose at a rate of 3.6% per annum between 1983 and 1987, but it rose at a rate of 17% from 1987 to 1992. The increases in labour and rental costs appear to be factors in the decline in the net profit rate after 1988.

Will further increases in labour wages and rental costs wipe out retail profits and eventually bring about a decline in the retail industry? Our answer to both is negative. Let us look at the wage factor and the rental factor separately. Wage rates largely depend on the overall demand and supply situation of the labour market. For retail industry workers, there is no well-defined "sub-market" which means that when the retail industry is growing, workers can enter the industry relatively easily; no long-term training is required. However, when the retail industry is contracting, workers can move out and join other industries. The lock-in effect is very small. As a result, the wage rates of retail workers follow the overall wage rates in the labour market. The period of rapid increase in wage rates observed in Table 6.3 coincided with a period of general tightness in the labour market. Even during these years, the increase in wage rates was not phenomenal. Moreover, labour costs accounted for just around 7% of total costs. So unless wage rates increase greatly, the impact of future tightness in the labour market is unlikely to have a huge impact on retail profits. Using 1992 figures as a benchmark, a 10% increase in wage rates, other prices kept constant, would have reduced net profit by about 11%. If we repeat the calculation using figures for earlier years, we would find that, over time, the sensitivity of net profit to wage rate in fact diminishes rather than increases.

Concerning rental rates, Table 6.3 might give the impression that rental rate increases squeezed net profits, but the direction of causation should be just the reverse. The rental rate for retail space depends entirely on supply and demand. The supply of retail space has been growing steadily. The increase in rental rates was most likely a demand-side phenomenon. The demand for retail space was strong because investors were attracted by the high profitability of the business. In other words, the landlord captured part of the profits of the retail business as rent. Rent is part of the residual of retail receipts over other retail costs. However, unlike retail workers, usage of retail space is locked-in; so rental rates are flexible downwards as well as upwards, depending on demand. Based on this line of reasoning, if the retail business declines, the rental rate of retail space should decline as well. High rental rates cannot, therefore, be a cause of low profit. Simply put, high rental rates are caused by high profits. Having said that, we need to remark that there could be some adjustment-friction in the short term. Lease contracts typically last two years or longer, and so rental rates are not instantaneously responsive to changes in demand. Until the lease contract expires, a downturn in business would put excessive pressure on profitability. Given the time for rental rates to adjust, however, the impact of rental cost on retail profitability is very small.[5]

Our analysis suggests that despite rising labour and rental costs, the retail industry has been earning steady profits. There should not be excessive worry over the future viability of the industry, for two reasons. First, operational cost is only moderately sensitive to wage rates, and there is no indication that wages rates will increase rapidly. Second, since rental costs follow from high profits and high demand for retail space, it is inconceivable that high rentals could drive out the retail industry.

Ingredients of Success

The retail industry in Hong Kong possesses several natural advantages. The first of these is its geographical location. A large number of people in the People's Republic of China are eager to shop in Hong Kong. Transport links by air, by land and by sea between the People's Republic of China and Hong Kong give Hong Kong a considerable advantage over other cities in the region. Hong Kong is also less than two hours away from Taipei, three hours away from Bangkok, and less than four hours away from

Singapore, Kuala Lumpur, and Tokyo. It is predicted that the region will be the fastest-growing area in the world in the next decade, and Hong Kong's retail industry stands to gain from the trend.[6] Hong Kong's second natural advantage is its cultural proximity to the People's Republic of China, Taiwan, and many Chinese nationals of the region. Hong Kong and these countries share common languages: Cantonese, Mandarin, and English. The ability to communicate in a common language with customers is an advantage. Many Hong Kong people speak two or more languages and dialects; and, in many retail stores, sales representatives can speak fluent Japanese too. Hong Kong's third advantage is its well-established infrastructure for retail businesses. The many well-designed and well-maintained shopping centres, the transportation and the banking networks, and other support services such as hotel and dining facilities, all make Hong Kong shopping a pleasant experience. While other cities may match Hong Kong in one or more of these advantages, it is hard to find another city that possesses all of them.

Despite these advantages, there is no guarantee that Hong Kong retailing can remain competitive in the long term. The major enemy is rising costs. Most of the things that visitors buy are not produced in Hong Kong. Hong Kong has no advantage in getting these goods at a particularly low cost. If retail costs in Hong Kong are high, it is conceivable that some other cities could replace Hong Kong as a shopping mecca.[7] What will be viable then?

The key to long-term viability is business volume. It is the nature of the retail business that sales receipts increase faster than do expenses. The constraint on higher profit is on the side of sales volume, rather than on the side of overhead costs. When sales volume is high, a retail shop is much better able to absorb high labour and rental costs. High business volume also has an impact at the industry level. Many shoppers can support many shops. Even if they sell goods in the same category, competition among shops would drive each of them to sell something different, maybe different brands or different models. High business volume drives variety, something that shoppers in Hong Kong value a great deal. Before making a purchase, shoppers can take a close look at the competition compare prices, quality and so on.

To maintain a high retail volume, Hong Kong needs two things, namely, significant growth in the number of visitors and improved efficiency. Maintaining significant growth in the number of visitors pertains to the development of tourism as a whole, requiring more airport capacity, sufficient air services, and economical supporting facilities. As for efficiency, each worker has to handle more business. The average productivity of retail workers must increase. Part of the solution lies in better management by introducing more worker training, better incentive schemes and better work routines. Another direction for improvement lies in better technology. There is much room for improvement in inventory checking, sales flow monitoring, sales analysis and store security. With the adoption of more advanced technology, a great deal of manpower presently devoted to these tasks could be saved and sales revenue per worker could be increased. Hong Kong already has a good infrastructure in information technology where computers, the Internet, an optical fibre network, and state-of-the-art telecommunication devices are already widely used, with electronic money to come very soon. Improving efficiency in the retail businesses will require better utilization of this infrastructure.

Notes

1. Singapore is also a popular tourist destination which has a well-established retail industry. Many of the international brand names that are carried in Hong Kong can also be found in Singapore. Yet there is no evidence suggesting that Singapore will undermine Hong Kong's retail industry. Large tourist traffic plus a large local demand for retail goods give Hong Kong an advantage in maximizing the variety and timeliness of merchandises.

2. There are established markets for goods of "pirate" brands in Hong Kong. They are sold in specific areas at deeply discounted prices. But consumers usually are not deceived. There have been few documented complaints that tourists have been cheated. Generally, they manage to get what they have paid for.

3. There is no denying that retailers do suffer losses as a result of mis-stocking. Nevertheless, as the stock turnover rate is typically high, the level of stock is usually kept low, mitigating the damage. Moreover, the markup for style goods is usually rather high, which helps restricting direct losses.

4. There has been no formal study on the rapid growth of cosmetics retailing in Hong Kong. One conjecture is the global cosmetic industry is very competitive, with a large number of brand names coming from the United States, France, Switzerland and Japan. Hong Kong has been able to utilize its international exposure to source these merchandises from around the world through hundreds of wholesalers.

5. As evidence, in the early 1980s when the economy was stagnant, overall growth and retail growth in particular, were slow. Retail rental declined from 1981 onwards, dropping 44% by 1984, and did not recover fully until 1988.

6. To increase retail purchases, more tourists have to be brought to Hong Kong. Relying on higher purchase per tourist is not a sustainable option.

7. Singapore could become a much stronger retail destination if retail purchases among local residents could be stimulated.

CHAPTER 7

Building New Attractions

Introduction

Famous cities like London and Paris have long histories of cultural development, offering tourists a wide variety of palaces and museums for sightseeing. This makes the cities inherently attractive to visitors. Hong Kong is less fortunate in this regard. It is commonly agreed that Hong Kong does not have a great deal to offer in terms of cultural heritage or natural scenery. Hong Kong is a place of business. When visitors are not cutting deals of some kind, they are usually dining in one of the city's 8,000 restaurants (including fast-food shops and bars) or shopping in one of its 50,000 retail outlets.

The scarcity of attractions besides eating establishments and shopping facilities has caused concern among tourism developers in Hong Kong. The general worry is that as prices in Hong Kong are rising, it will soon lose its reputation as a "shopper's paradise". Moreover, as countries in the region are getting richer and more liberal, more direct flights will be developed, and this would hurt Hong Kong in its capacity as a transport hub. It has also been observed that some countries in the region, such as Singapore, have grand visions of turning their cities into tourism magnets. These cities are drawing up big investment plans for developing tourism amenities. In short, the concern among tourism developers is over how Hong Kong can maintain its attractiveness in the midst of rising costs, falling volume of *en route* traffic, and increasing regional competition.

Table 7.1

Percentage of Visitors Having Visited the Major Tourist Attractions, 1995

Country of Residence	Victoria Peak (1)	Repulse Bay (2)	Ocean Park (3)	Aberdeen (4)	Stanley (5)	Open-Air Market (6)	W.T.S. Temple (7)	A.B.H. Gardens (8)	Outer Islands (9)
Japan / South Korea	59	35	7	34	21	17	13	32	2
Taiwan	29	15	32	12	7	8	16	5	4
South & S. E. Asia	30	20	30	17	10	16	8	1	6
Australia, New Zealand, & Pacific	44	25	9	28	38	27	3	1	11
Americas	50	31	4	33	34	25	7	1	9
Europe, Africa, & Middle East	63	36	9	47	38	30	10	3	16
Mainland China	41	27	57	16	1	3	19	12	18
All Countries	45	27	26	25	16	15	13	11	9

Source: *Visitor Profile Report 1995,* HKTA.

Note: See Figure 7.1 for proximate locations of attractions which are identified by the column numbers. See also text for names.

The Hong Kong Tourist Association (HKTA), a government-funded organization charged with the responsibility of promoting tourism in Hong Kong, has generated far-reaching ideas to boost Hong Kong's tourism superstructure. Most of these ideas are still at the conceptual stage. In appraising their merits, a number of strategic questions have to be answered. Basic questions to be raised are, first, how are these projects going to be financed and how is the necessary land going to be acquired; and second, whether the new attractions will complement Hong Kong's strengths in view of the resources available in the People's Republic of China.

Where Do Visitors Go?

To start with, we take a look at the places in Hong Kong that visitors go to most often. We can identify nine of the most popular tourist spots, and Table 7.1 shows their popularity among visitors

Figure 7.1
Locations of Attractions

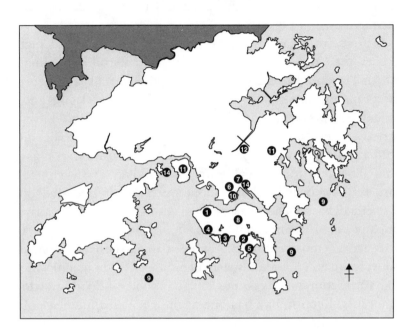

from different source markets in 1995. The last row of Table 7.1 shows the proportion of all travellers who visited each of the nine spots. As one traveller might have visited more than one of the spots, the percentages do not add up to 100. It appears that Victoria Peak was the most popular spot overall, as 45% of all visitors went there in 1995. The second most popular place was Repulse Bay, at 27%, and the third most popular place was the Ocean Park, at 26%, followed closely by Aberdeen, at 25%. The other five spots were significantly less popular. In order of decreasing popularity, they were Stanley (16%), the open-air market (15%), the Wong Tai Sin Temple (13%), the Aw Boon Haw (Tiger Balm) Gardens (11%), and the outlying islands (9%).

There are interesting differences between the preferences of visitors from different source markets. Visitors can be divided into three groups. The first group consists of visitors from Japan and South Korea; the second group consists of visitors from Taiwan,

Southeast Asia, and the People's Republic of China; and the third group consists of visitors from Australia, New Zealand, the Pacific, the Americas, and Europe.

Visitors from Japan and South Korea generally had higher incomes than did some other visitors, and they liked going to Victoria Peak, Aberdeen, and Repulse Bay. Victoria Peak offers the world-famous bird's-eye view of much of Hong Kong and is particularly spectacular at night. It is also close to the business districts, where most first-class hotels are situated. The most popular spot there was the shopping centre, which also serves as the terminal building for the peak tram. The building was developed by a private developer, and the shopping centre is operated on a commercial basis. The peak tram is also operated by a private company on a commercial basis. Traffic volume is low, and passengers are mostly tourists. Aberdeen used to be a fishing village. Today, tourists can find only a small number of fishing junks there, and its attraction mainly comes from a number of floating seafood restaurants. Repulse Bay has one of the better-maintained public beaches in Hong Kong. It also boasts a number of luxury restaurants that have a distinct colonial flavour. All three places are rather close to the business districts. A bit surprising, at least to the average Hong Kong person, is that about one-third of the Japanese and Korean visitors visited the Aw Boon Haw Gardens. Residents seldom go there any more. The Gardens are nevertheless on the standard itineraries of many tour groups from Japan and Korea. The place is not particularly well maintained and is definitely not representative of the living style of Hong Kong people. Its principal advantage is in its location, which is right in the middle of town, and it therefore serves as a convenient city tour stopover point and a good place to take photographs.[1] The data therefore suggest that most Japanese and Korean visitors stayed within the hotel and shopping areas. Commuting time is an important consideration and should not be overlooked in the development of new facilities.

The second group, which consisted of visitors from Taiwan, Southeast Asia, and the People's Republic of China, were quite different from the first group. They were predominantly Chinese, and, on average, they were not as wealthy as the Japanese and the Korean. Although tourists from China also visited Victoria Peak, Aberdeen, and Repulse Bay, among their group, the most popular place was the Ocean Park, an important destination on the itineraries of most seven-day Hong Kong tours sold to People's Republic of China visitors. It was interesting to them because it was a new experience for most people from the People's Republic of China and Taiwan. The place is large and relaxed, and most Chinese visitors did not have any problem getting around. Nevertheless, the place is also rather time-consuming, and therefore only repeat visitors or those not in a hurry would consider going there. The Wong Tai Sin Temple, interestingly enough, was also a popular tourism spot among this group. Revered by locals, the Wong Tai Sin Temple is a place that many people believe can make wishes come true. For this reason, perhaps, many visitors from Taiwan and the People's Republic of China also went there.

Visitors from the West, who formed the third group, were distinctly different. While they also went to Victoria Peak, Aberdeen, and Repulse Bay, few went to the Aw Boon Haw Gardens, the Wong Tai Sin Temple, or the Ocean Park. Instead, they visited Stanley and the open-air market, and a significant proportion of them went to the outlying islands. The open-air market is almost a flea market, and Stanley resembles a tropical fishing village with a line-up of street stalls selling handicrafts, souvenirs, and low-priced clothing. The people in this group are not usually shoppers, like the first group, and they were not attracted by the Wong Tai Sin Temple and the Ocean Park as much as the second group was. A significant number of them did visit the outlying islands, however, which represent the less crowded and more natural side of Hong Kong.

From the tourism developer's perspective, there are three groups of *potential* visitors. These are the targets of further tourism development. First, there are travellers who have never visited Hong Kong. There has been no systematic and comprehensive study, although it would be worthwhile to conduct one, investigating why these travellers have not chosen Hong Kong as a

Table 7.2

Seven Major Projects under Study by the HKTA

Project	Location	Time frame
(10) Hong Kong Exposition	South East Kowloon	1996–2001
(11) Film City	Tsing Yi or Sai Kung	1999–2004
(12) Aquatic Centre	Shatin	1997–1998
(13) Cruise Centre	Urban Core	2004–2011
(14) Theme Park	Tsing Ma or S. E. Kowloon	1999–2004
(15) Festival Market Place	Urban Core	1999–2010
(16) New Peak	Urban Core	1999–2010

Source: Hong Kong Tourist Association

Note: See Figure 7.1 for proximate locations which are identified by the row
          numbers; but projects (13), (15) and (16) in the urban core are not shown.

travel destination. For first-time visitors, Hong Kong still offers many exciting experiences. More marketing efforts overseas may help boost the popularity of Hong Kong. Additional tourist attractions will also draw more first-time visitors. Second, there are travellers who visit Hong Kong repeatedly, most of them being business travellers and shoppers. They are not looking for facilities such as Ocean Park. What appeals to them may be efficient urban transport, good hotels, and good restaurants. Third, there are those travellers who have been to Hong Kong once, but cannot find a reason to make a second visit. This is the major target group for which new tourist attractions are being planned. More research should be conducted to studying the characteristics and preferences of this last group of visitors, as understanding their needs is essential to the future planning of tourist attractions.

HKTA Initiatives

In view of the shortage of tourist attractions in Hong Kong, the HKTA has generated a number of ideas for making Hong Kong more interesting to travellers. As a non-profit organization funded by the government the Association promotes the tourism trade via a worldwide network of offices that maintain close contact with tourist agencies overseas. Recently, the HKTA has been taking on an increasingly important role in the development of tourism infrastructure. It has drawn up plans for seven major projects for the consideration of the government and the public. These projects are summarized in Table 7.2.

The first project is Hong Kong Expo. The intention is to use the present Kai Tak airport site to stage a large scale exhibition in 2001 to mark the opening of the next millennium. The exhibition will combine a showcase of Hong Kong and People's Republic of China products with entertainment and cultural events. Its purpose will be to establish Hong Kong as China's window to the world — a business hub where people from the East and West meet. This objective is especially important to some people who fear that other cities in the People's Republic of China, such as Shanghai, might one day replace Hong Kong as China's business hub.

The second project is Film City, to be built on Tsing Yi Island or in Sai Kung. It will be modelled after Universal Studios in California. Here, visitors will be able to see firsthand the working sets and costumes from some well-known movies produced in Hong Kong. Hong Kong is the world's third-largest producer of movies, after the United States and India. Hong Kong movies are exported to the People's Republic of China, Taiwan, and many countries in Southeast Asia. In recent years, an increasing number of movies have been exported to North America and Europe, where the population of Chinese immigrants is growing.

The third project is an aquatic centre to be built in Shatin. The aquatic centre will consist of world-class facilities for the staging of rowing and canoeing events. When no such events are taking place, the facility will be used for water skiing and other water sports. The international dragon boat races, which take place every year in Victoria Harbour, will find a permanent home here. This facility requires two kilometres of unobstructed and quiet waterway and land for the building of a spectator stand and parking facilities.

The fourth project is a cruise centre. The idea is to build a modern berthing facility and passenger terminal, complete with shopping, dining, and hotel facilities as well as transport links.

Cruise passengers are usually wealthy travellers. Elsewhere in the region, the Singaporean government has already taken steps to capture this market. A cruise centre in Singapore will be completed soon.

The fifth project is a theme park. Possible locations are Tsing Ma, which is close to the new airport and transport links, and Southeast Kowloon, the present Kai Tak airport site. The theme park will resemble Disneyland in California, which offers games, adventure, entertainment, shopping, and restaurants.

The sixth project is a festival marketplace to be built in the urban core. It is to resemble Covent Garden in London. It is intended to be a waterfront centre that provides facilities for shopping, food, and live entertainment.

The seventh project is a new peak location to be run alongside the existing one. It will provide an additional vantage point for visitors to enjoy the harbour and city view. A funicular transport link to allow direct access to and from the urban area is also planned.

The government is keeping an open mind about these project proposals. In the budget speech of 1996, the Financial Secretary announced that it would award the HKTA a HK$8 million grant for pursuing feasibility studies on these projects. When the studies are completed, the matter will be actively discussed by the government, the HKTA, private enterprises, and the public.

The major question to be considered in the appraisal of the seven projects is that of how they are going to be financed. The usual government position is to keep government involvement in such ventures to a minimum. The government's basic task is to ensure that a development is consistent with the long-term land-use planning of the development site. Even for large projects, the involvement of the government has been limited to the provision of a land grant. The cost of the development and the management of the facility are in most cases the responsibility of the private enterprise. The developer has to appraise a project on the basis of its return to investment. Among the popular tourist spots, small-scale developments such as Stanley, Victoria Peak, Aberdeen, and

Repulse Bay (excluding the beach, which is maintained by the government) were developed by private enterprises on profit grounds. Ocean Park, which is a large-scale development, was built by the Hong Kong Jockey Club using money extracted from betting turnover and is run by an independent management company under the authority of the Urban Council. The land on which the park was built was, however, granted by the government.

The government's philosophy has not been accepted without question. The government has clearly played a large role in the building of the new airport. Both the new airport and the proposed tourist attractions can draw tourists, which benefits the Hong Kong economy. The question arises as to where the line of minimal government involvement is to be drawn. There is, however, a more compelling argument for minimal government involvement. In running a facility, the government is not as flexible and customer oriented as a private enterprise is. The government is usually not able to charge prices in accordance with market conditions, because the public can easily see the facility as a part of the social infrastructure. If long-run viability and the quality of service are prime considerations, then the government is right in keeping involvement to a minimum. Many studies around the world have also suggested that businesses improved in efficiency, profitability, and quality of service after they had been privatized.

There are two major concerns. First, are the projects in the best interests of Hong Kong? The question arises because the projects require substantial land which is a very valuable resource in Hong Kong. Most of the projects require that land be acquired at below-market rates. Second, is there sufficient interest among private enterprises to make the project work? It is likely that innovative financing methods will be essential for the success of theses projects. These considerations are discussed in greater detail below.

Identifying Strengths

Whether the project in question is a development such as Film City or a theme park, the acquisition of sufficient land is a prerequisite.

In addition, the land site has to be supported by sufficient infrastructure — roads, water supply, sewerage, and so on. Even if a
project is entirely privately-financed, public funds are involved in a
direct or indirect way. The site could be used for many alternative
purposes. On a general level, the building of a large facility is not a
localized matter. It is a matter of resource use at the economy level.

As a general observation, if one looks at large cities in developed
countries, tourism attractions are rarely built from scratch. Places
like Disneyland and Universal Studios attract many tourists from
other cities in the United States and from abroad. Yet they were not
built with the intention of earning tourism revenue.[2] In New York,
visitors who do not come for business go to see the architecture, the
monuments, the museums, and the shopping centres. In London
and Paris, as in many other European cities, the main attractions are
palaces, memorials, cathedrals, and museums. Again, they were not
built to earn tourism revenue. Tourism facility building seems to be
a recent innovation that has taken hold among industrializing
countries in Asia in particular. Many of the ideas for tourism
facilities were put forward for the purpose of using tourism as a
foreign exchange earner.

The projects to be undertaken in Hong Kong should complement Hong Kong's strengths. Even an existing facility that fails to
meet this criterion will be unable to withstand competition from
other cities. Other cities could, in all likelihood, build a very similar
attraction at a fraction of the cost. Take for example the Splendid
China miniature scenic spot in Shenzhen. Here visitors can see
miniature versions of many of the best-known scenes in China such
as the Great Wall, the Qinling Mausoleum, the Zhaozhou Bridge,
the Imperial Palace, the Potala Palace, the Three Gorges, the Shao-
lin Temple, and scores of others. The entire development spans
hundreds of acres. It is financed and run by private interests in
China. A park of this size could not be viable in Hong Kong. If Hong
Kong is to build a theme park, potential competition from other cities has to be seriously considered. Even if Hong Kong can achieve a
higher quality of service, the difference in set-up and running costs,
and the abundance of resources elsewhere, are overwhelming

factors working against the success of such a project. To be success-ful, the theme park has to capture a concept that cannot be easily reproduced elsewhere.

The same considerations apply to other proposed projects, as well. The Hong Kong Expo must incorporate activities and exhibits that only Hong Kong can put up; otherwise people will not find it interesting. Film City must build on a number of world-famous movies that were produced in Hong Kong or by Hong Kong. The aquatic centre must stage frequent international events to make it attractive to visitors. Likewise, the cruise centre must offer something that other passenger piers in the region cannot, especially as Singapore is already building such a centre. Closely related is the festival marketplace, which should have a character of its own and should not be just another line-up of restaurants and retail outlets. Incidentally, Stanley, blocks in Kowloon known as "Bird Street" and "Women's Street", the jade market, Lan Kwai Fong, and the antique stores in uptown Central are unique places that nevertheless developed without much deliberate planning, let alone government direction.

Also important to consider is the cost to visitors of extending the length of their stay in Hong Kong. In question is not the entrance fee to the planned facilities but the extra accommodation cost and living expenses required for a longer stay. The average length of stay is slightly more than three days. At present, most tourist attractions are close to the hotel districts, and a tour of all of them may take just half a day. The rest of a visitor's time is spent on shopping. It may not be easy to lure visitors away from the urban core to visit Film City, say, which is to be located in the New Territories.

One concept that is well worth stressing is that of Chinese ethnicity. Some 40% of visitors to Hong Kong in 1995 came from Taiwan and Mainland China. A large number of those who came from other countries also have a Chinese background, although the exact number of these is not known. This trend will continue well into the future. These visitors have a profound appreciation for Chinese culture. By virtue of Hong Kong's international exposure, articles and ideas appealing to people interested in Chinese culture can be brought to Hong Kong from all over the world. Attractions may range from Chinese movies to Chinese music; Chinese literature; Chinese antiques, handicrafts, and artwork; and the celebrities, artists, etc. who produce all these things. In this area, Hong Kong has an advantage no other city possesses.[3]

Financing

The proposed projects will basically be privately financed. Some donations may be forthcoming from charitable organizations like the Hong Kong Jockey Club and certain private foundations, but the bulk of the investment has to come from private enterprises. What this means is that each project will have to be appraised as a commercial initiative.

To start with, none of these projects can be commercially viable if land is acquired at the market rate. The logic here is that if a development is commercially viable, it should have already been taken on by one of the many real estate companies. If a facility does not already exist, the obstacle in most cases is one of land availability. Land supply is a broad issue in Hong Kong. It concerns the revenue that the government receives from land sales which has been a significant source of government revenue, the overall level of land prices, and the allocation of the limited amount of land to residential, commercial, and industrial uses.

Some innovative financing methods have to be devised in order for the projects described above to work. One method that merits consideration is packaging several projects into a single development. Take the festival marketplace as an example. The government can designate a site on which it is to be developed. It can plan a hotel, an exhibition hall, and an office building in the same complex. The government can then build these parameters into a single land-lease and development permit. By specifying an assortment of activities in one complex, the attractiveness of each individual component can be enhanced, and the land will fetch a higher price. Such specifications will also ensure that there will be sufficient interest in developing the festival marketplace, which by itself may not be a lucrative proposition. The same idea may be applied to Film City or to the theme park. Both Film City and the theme park may not, by themselves, be very attractive to private developers. Adding the right to develop a hotel in the park into the land lease may sweeten the deal quite a lot. Of course, in the event that developers are willing to put up a lower bid than they otherwise would be, the government is indirectly subsidizing the park. Nevertheless, if the hotel adds value to the park because of easier access, and the park adds value to the hotel because of customer flow, an indirect subsidy does not necessarily arise.

The development of the Gold Coast in Tuen Mun is a prime example of such a situation. Before development, the area was not much more than a small, forgotten beach. The development right of the area was then granted through auction to a private developer. Today, there are dozens of high-rise residential buildings, a luxury hotel, a yacht club, a large shopping complex with many shops, and an attractive waterfront promenade. None of the facilities would have been feasible in isolation.

All the proposed HKTA projects have one thing in common. They have very high start-up costs and relatively low running costs. The commercial viability of such businesses depends critically on customer volume. The customer volume has to be high enough not only to cover running costs and provide a reasonable return to initial investment but also to allow a surplus to upgrade service and provide for reinvestment. In the case of some of the proposed projects, tourists alone may not generate sufficient revenue. The key is therefore to generate sufficient interest among locals. As the proposed projects are diverse in nature, it is hard to generalize about the level of local interest expected. Film City may be interesting to locals in the beginning, but unless there are frequent new additions, interest will die rather quickly, and most customers will not make repeat visits. The success of the aquatic centre in particular will depend critically on local interest, as there is a limit to the number of international events that can be staged there. To be attractive to locals, it must offer substantially better service than the existing facilities. The cruise centre cannot derive its main business from cruise passengers. There are not enough of them in the region. It must offer something unique, something that attracts local customers away from the usual shopping centres. The theme park, like Film City, must continuously add new attractions to generate a constant flow of local visitors. It must also differentiate itself from Ocean Park, which, among other things, also offers amusement park excitement. Similarly, in order to attract local customers, the festival marketplace must offer more than just ordinary shopping, food and beverage, and entertainment facilities. These things are already available at a number of shopping centres on both sides of the harbour. Providing something unique is a challenge deserving of thought and attention.[4]

Notes

1. More than 80% of Japanese vacation visitors in 1995 came in packaged-tour groups.

2. Today, Universal Studios is mainly a tourist-oriented attraction. Little actual filming is being undertaken there.

3. When a substantial number of new attractions are in place, there will be significant diversification away from shopping, resulting in a more balanced mix of tourism activities. As the new attractions are still at a planning stage, it is prudent to predict that shopping will continue to be the core activity for five years or more.

4. "Industrial tourism" is an interesting concept, wherein tourists observe industrial activities in action. Examples of suitable venue are fashion factories, porcelain factories, restaurant kitchens, movie sites, orchestra rehearsal halls, art studios, horse-racing courses, and so on. The author wishes to thank an anonymous referee for pointing out this concept.

CHAPTER 8

Policy Recommendations

Introduction

The tourism business in Hong Kong faces no imminent danger. Hong Kong's inherent strengths — proximity to China, business volume, financial centre status, shopping and dining facilities, and a stylish metropolitan setting — will continue to draw visitors from the Asia-Pacific region and the rest of the world. There is, however, a need to enhance the competitiveness of Hong Kong tourism. In the first place, as Hong Kong moves towards a service-oriented economy, tourism stands out as one of the few sectors that can drive economic growth through exporting services. The tourism sector in Hong Kong is still small relative to the manufacturing and financial sectors. There is certainly opportunity for the sector to assume a larger role in the economy. Second, competition in the region is mounting. Cities such as Seoul, Bangkok, and Singapore are ready to launch aggressive plans to develop tourism. Singapore, in particular, is studying the tourism sector systematically to evaluate its potential as a growth driver.[1] A recently published report highlights a number of initiatives that may serve as a useful reference for Hong Kong.

While detailed proposals are beyond the scope of this book, a number of strategic directions for further consideration may be pointed out here.

First of all, Hong Kong needs to adopt an integrative mindset in its approach to tourism. A fragmented mindset would see airlines, airports, trains, hotels, restaurants, shopping centres, and urban amenities as disparate "businesses". In the mind of many people, that these are *integrated* components of tourism is often overlooked. The power of tourism to drive economic growth has not been well recognized.

Second, there should be policies that would make Hong Kong more accessible to the world. Such policies may include allowing more flights to Hong Kong, continuous expansion of airport capacity, more efficient customs and immigration clearance, and more efficient visa issuance.

Third, innovative methods of tapping into China's resources should be sought. The China factor is one area that will loom large in the future of Hong Kong tourism. Apart from more inbound tourists from the provinces, China's rich, untouched natural habitats and rich cultural heritage offer great opportunities for Hong Kong to bring the world to these treasures. The Pearl River Delta concept being promoted at present is an important step in the appropriate direction.

Fourth, Hong Kong can make itself more attractive as a tourist location. The government should carefully regulate the supply of hotels. It should also attract private participation in the building of new tourist attractions.

Finally, more efforts should be devoted to environmental protection and enhancement. A healthy and pleasing environment will not only make Hong Kong more attractive as a tourist destination but will also improve the quality of living of Hong Kong residents. Now, in order to put these five directions in a regional-competition perspective, it would be useful to dissect the 1996 Singaporean tourism strategy in terms of its four specific directions.

The Singaporean Strategy

A number of cities in the Asia-Pacific region are making large strides in developing tourism. Singapore is perhaps the city making the most systematic and aggressive efforts. The direction in which Singapore is moving can serve as a useful reference for other aspiring cities.

The driving force behind Singapore's tourism development is the Singapore Tourist Promotion Board, which is similar in nature to the Hong Kong Tourist Association (HKTA). The Singapore Tourist Promotion Board works closely with the World Travel and Tourism Council in promoting global tourism. The World Travel and Tourism Council is a London-based coalition of chief executive officers from various tourism sectors (hotels, airlines, car rental agencies, travel agencies, and so on) around the world. The chief executive officer of Singapore Airlines, which is controlled by the Singaporean government, is an executive committee member of the coalition. In October 1996 the coalition issued a report on the role of tourism in Singapore and the strategic directions for development. The document will be used to steer the setting up of detailed policies in Singapore.

According to the report, travel and tourism in Singapore accounted for 12% of the GDP in 1996. Travel and tourism provided employment for 162,000 workers in 1996. The number of employees in this sector has fluctuated quite widely over the last decade. The first setback came in 1991, when it dropped from 175,000 in 1990 to 134,000 in 1991. The second setback came in 1993, when the number dropped from 158,000 in 1992 to 125,000 in 1993. The third setback, albeit a minor one, came in 1996, when the number dropped from 179,000 in 1995 to 162,000 in 1996. These fluctuations cannot be attributed to global downturns, for employment in the travel and tourism industries worldwide has been on the increase in every year of the past decade. It appears that inter-city competition has been intensifying. Only cities that are able to maintain an ongoing competitive edge can hope to keep a constant share of the global market. The volatility of the business should be taken into consideration in any development programme. In particular, capacity expansion of tourist facilities such as hotels and amusement parks should be undertaken in accordance with long-term trends rather than with short-term fluctuations.

Singapore has made tourism development a high priority. The Singapore Tourism Promotion Board has developed a set of statistics that show the contribution of travel and tourism to the economy, taking into account the different components of the sector. Such statistics are not available in Hong Kong. Singapore also recognizes the important role of travel and tourism as the nation moves towards a knowledge-intensive, service-oriented economy.

The October 1996 report highlights four strategic directions for tourism development. These directions will form the framework for policy initiatives in Singapore in the next decade.

Make Travel and Tourism a Strategic Development and Employment Priority

1. Recognize the importance of the travel and tourism sector and accord it a central role in the formulation of government policies over "job creation, export promotion, and investment stimulation".
2. Set up a National Satellite Account for travel and tourism in accordance with United Nations standards to show the flow of value in the economy created by businesses from the sector.

The Singaporean government is very adept at directing national resources to fulfill policy goals. It has been successful in the past in attracting foreign direct investment in high-technology industries. There are unverifiable reports claiming that the Singaporean government has used subsidies to compete for major international conferences. In the coming decade, Singapore will emerge as a very competitive tourist location.

Take Steps towards Creating Open and Competitive Markets

1. "Support the implementation of the General Agreement on Trade in Services" by liberalizing air service and international telecommunication service.
2. Improve the quality of Singapore travel and tourism service in order to "compete more effectively for visitors".

Singapore has been advocating a more liberal aviation industry in Asia for many years. Indeed, Singapore has much to gain from liberalization. It has a large airport that is under-utilized. It has one of the world's most efficient and profitable airlines. The economy of Singapore is rather small, about half the size of that of Hong Kong, and so it depends heavily on transit and *en route* traffic. If Singapore pursues the aviation hub status with sufficient conviction, some traffic in the region will be diverted there.

Pursue Environmentally Sustainable Development

Land and resources are scarce in Singapore. There is a great deal of concern over the possibility that the infrastructural development necessitated by foreign direct investment and tourism promotion might harm the environment. Addressing this concern is one of Singapore's major challenges, and the environmental perspective is always taken into consideration in major policy decisions. To the extent that environmentalism is a world trend, efforts to enhance the environment should also play a role in the future infrastructural development of Hong Kong.

Remove Bottlenecks to the Growth of Travel and Tourism

1. Expand the airport, roads, and other infrastructures.
2. Implement automated border clearance.
3. Lower taxes and user charges levied at airport, hotels, and restaurants.
4. Train better workers.

Removing bottlenecks is an important component of development planning. Compared to Hong Kong, Singapore has tended to build capacity ahead of its time. The advantage is that bottlenecks in airports, hotels, or the road system have been largely avoided. This advantage comes at a cost, however. Much of the infrastructure was under-utilized for a long period, which deters private participation in the construction of infrastructure. Consequently, unlike the Hong Kong government, the Singaporean government has to finance most infrastructure. The automated border clearance system known as Future Automated Screening for Travelers (FAST) being studied in Singapore is a high-technology system that works on biometric identification for rapid and reliable visitor screening. This system allows the airport to handle a large number of travellers rapidly. Although the system may not be appropriate for Hong Kong, speeding up the process of security checks and visa clearance could be an important aspect of tourism development. Taxes and user charges are light in both Singapore and Hong Kong. In both cities, taxes and user charges are not important considerations for the time being. The last initiative, that of worker training, could figure prominently in Singapore, judging by the heavy investment in worker training that it has made in producing sufficient engineers for the use of foreign technology companies. Whether the Hong Kong government should play the same key role is debatable. In Hong Kong, the training of workers in the travel and tourism sector has been largely the task of the private operators. The government cannot train workers to the same degree of specificity as can the operators themselves. The government does not have the ability to select those workers that operators find most suitable for particular positions. In Hong Kong, the task of worker training is best left to the operators.

The Future Direction of Hong Kong Tourism

The Singapore experience is presented here not to suggest that Hong Kong should copy their initiatives. The intention is rather to give some indication as to the extent of the competition with which Hong Kong will be faced. Other cities in the region, such as Bangkok and Seoul, are launching plans similar to Singapore's. What can Hong Kong do to maintain its competitiveness?

What should the role of the government be? Unlike the indisputable role that a government should play in providing general education, security, health services, and enforcement of legal rights, the appropriate role of government in tourism development is one of a facilitator rather than an investor or an operator.

What if a government actively function as investors and operators? When the government is an investor, it is really investing public funds. Because a government also has multiple objectives other than tourism promotion, it cannot invest on the principle of maximizing investment return. The return to government investment tends to be lower than the return to private investment, which, save for cases involving substantial social returns, would lead to misallocation of investment funds. When the government is an operator, it can rarely set prices in accordance with market conditions, which frequently leads to permanent subsidies and low service quality. The third role, the government being a facilitator is appropriate and important. The government needs to have a sense of the direction that the economy is heading and to create initiatives to take advantage of trends. These initiatives need not involve much expenditure. They act to lead the private sector and to co-ordinate the diverse objectives of different private enterprises.

In a more positive vein, the Hong Kong government should facilitate the development of tourism by establishing an integrative mindset throughout Hong Kong concerning tourism, by making Hong Kong more accessible to visitors, by exploring the advantages of the China factor, and by spearheading projects that make Hong Kong more attractive.

The Integrative Mindset

Of foremost importance in the development of tourism is the recognition of it as a major driver of economic growth. Hong Kong needs to develop an integrative mindset in assessing the impact of tourism and to formulate ways to nurture tourism business. An integrative mindset does not come naturally to most people, because the tourism business cuts across many industries, and in each of the industries visitors and residents tend to share the services provided. Industries and facilities such as airlines, airports, hotels, restaurants, retail outlets, transport modes, Ocean Park, and

Repulse Bay are utilized by residents as much as by visitors. There is no industry in Hong Kong that exclusively serves visitors.

The multifaceted nature of tourism underlies the fragmented treatment that it receives by the government. Tourism as an export service receives some attention from both the Trade and Industry Branch and the Economic Services Branch. Air Services Agreements are primarily the responsibility of the Economic Services Branch. Operations at the airport, including the scheduling of landing and take-off time slots, are the responsibility of the Civil Aviation Department (which will be replaced by the Aviation Authority at the new airport). The issuance of visas and border clearance procedures are handled by the Immigration Department. The zoning of land for the development of hotels is largely determined by the Planning Department. The promotion of tourism to travel agencies overseas is primarily the work of the Hong Kong Tourist Association (HKTA), a non-profit organization funded by the government. Some tourism facilities are run by independent organizations. Ocean Park, for example, is run by an independent agency under the Urban Council. The Convention and Exhibition Centre, which is the main venue for the organization of international conferences, is owned by the Trade Development Council and run by a private management company. It is important for these diverse organizations to realize that in terms of tourism development, their objectives are the same. There should be more co-ordination and information sharing between these organizations in order to realize their common goals.[2]

Making Hong Kong More Accessible

When a visitor comes to Hong Kong, he or she incurs a number of costs which depend on airfares, ease of booking flights, ease of obtaining visas, speed of border clearance, cost of hotels, and so on. Hong Kong would benefit if these costs are reduced.

To reduce airfare to Hong Kong there must be more competition among airlines. To increase the volume of air service to Hong Kong more flights must be allowed to land there. The realization of both of these objectives will mean that Hong Kong must "open its sky". Relying on increased flights within the confines of third and fourth freedoms[3] will not suffice, because consent of foreign airlines is essential. The most direct way to expand the volume of air service to Hong Kong and to promote competition among airlines is to grant fifth-freedom rights more freely to foreign airlines. This would allow more foreign airlines to enter the Hong Kong route markets.

The call for fifth-freedom liberalization is not new, and the benefits that such liberalization would bring to Hong Kong are well known. The obstacle to change is the redistribution of income that would result. Investors in the designated Hong Kong airlines may lose as their markets are opened to stronger competition. At the same time though, resident travellers and investors in tourism-related businesses may gain. The cost to the government of bringing about such a change is large. Nevertheless, some form of air rights liberalization in the region will likely occur in the next decade. Those cities that are overly conservative will lose out as traffic is diverted away. Hong Kong should liberalize sooner rather than later.

Airport capacity is going to be one of Hong Kong's major strengths. The new airport will provide sufficient capacity — and the room to expand — to allow Hong Kong to maintain its regional hub status. To adapt to Hong Kong's elevated status, immigration and customs clearance systems should be continuously updated by applying newest technologies to speed up passenger flow.

Hotel capacity is a tricky issue. On one hand, the more hotel rooms there are, the lower hotel rates will be; so to increase the flow of visitors, there should be more hotels. This logic implies that the government should zone more sites for the building of hotels. The complication in reality is that land is zoned for commercial premises, which means that a piece of commercial land may be used to construct either office buildings or hotels. When the return of hotel investment is small relative to that of office building investment, developers might choose to convert hotels into office buildings. Taking this complication into consideration, the suggestion by tourism developers is that some land sites should be zoned specifically for hotels so as to lock in the supply of hotel rooms. On the other hand, increasing the land area for hotels would push up the price of land zoned for other uses because its supply is reduced; land shortage for offices and factories would decrease Hong Kong's competitiveness. Another problem is that locking in certain sites for hotels would only reduce the value of these sites on the market. As land revenue constitutes a substantial portion of government revenue, this change in policy would adversely affect the government budget. The issue of the supply of hotel rooms is far-reaching, and it inevitably involves a great deal of balancing between gains and losses among various sectors of the economy.

As is suggested in Chapter 5, the best compromise is for the government to maintain a steady increase of hotel supply in accordance with the long-term growth of tourism. Establishing a "hotel use" zoning category is a step in the right direction. Moderate growth in hotel capacity will ensure that hotel operators earn sufficient profits and make refurbishment feasible. Regular maintenance is essential to sustaining the quality of service. Even though the land revenue of the government may be reduced, the loss has to be balanced against the gains that may result from a stronger tourism sector.

The China Factor

There are two aspects of the China factor. First, a large number of tourists from China will come to Hong Kong or will travel through Hong Kong on their way to other places. The increased tourist flow is a trend that is driven by the rising income of China residents and the gradual integration of China with the rest of the world. Hong Kong should take steps to enhance this flow of tourists.

The second aspect of the China factor concerns the resources that China has in attracting tourists from countries overseas. Hong Kong should play an active role in organizing tours to such destinations. Special attention should be paid to catering "cultural tours" to the needs of the millions of overseas Chinese and to developing new forms of "eco-tourism".

In terms of logistics, going to China through Hong Kong will continue to be the best approach for some time. The Pearl River Delta concept, which is being promoted worldwide, is a development in the right direction. The concept could also be extended to places further inland. In the past, China has been very strict about allowing foreigners, including Hong Kong businesses, to open travel agencies in China. There are signs that control will gradually relax. In the future Hong Kong businesses can tap this market by setting up agencies in China or by forming alliances with China enterprises. Another approach is to exhibit historical relics on loan from China in Hong Kong. The exhibition facilities and their management in Hong Kong are still far better than are their counterparts in China.

Besides historical treasures, China has many unspoiled natural habitats. Gaining in popularity among tourists from the West are the so-called "eco-tours", which involve visits to natural environments that are untouched by human civilization. Many countries in the region are developing eco-tours, and competition is going to be intense. China, with its wide-ranging climatic zones and extensive land coverage, will always have some fresh experience to offer.

Making Hong Kong More Attractive

There is certainly room for Hong Kong to become more attractive to visitors. Coming up for intense scrutiny will be the development projects proposed by the HKTA. The central issue is the extent that public money should be involved in financing the projects. Without some financial support from the government, most of them will not be able to get off the ground. One mild form of government subsidy that is worth considering is the "bundled land sale" arrangement whereby a tourist facility (which by itself may not be profitable to investors) would be bundled with another development (which is very profitable by itself) and be sold as an entire package at a land auction. If the two developments complement each other, then the price that the investors are willing to pay for the package would not be much reduced, and the government's subsidy would be correspondingly small. The Gold Coast Development in Tuen Mun is an example of such a package. This development, which was undertaken by a private developer on auctioned land, combined a hotel, a yacht club, and dozens of residential blocks together with a seaside promenade.

Finally, a wish is shared by residents and tourism developers alike is that the quality of the environment should steadily improve. The trend towards relocating manufacturing to China is favourable for Hong Kong in this regard. Yet air pollution caused by heavy car traffic and construction works, and water pollution caused by urbanization and land reclamation, remain problems that will require substantial investment to solve. A healthy and pleasing environment will surely make Hong Kong more attractive as a tourist destination. The quality of living of Hong Kong residents will improve too. Cleaning up Hong Kong deserves more government attention.

Notes

1. See the discussion on its tourism strategy in the following section.

2. The organizational structure that can bring about better coordination among the various agencies may take several forms. The important point is that the government has to take the initiative to establish the formal connections and to sustain the dedication to reach the common goal.

3. See Chapter 4 (p. 65) for an explanation of different levels of access in terms of five "freedoms".

Bibliography

1. Airport Authority (1996). *Airport Authority Annual Report 1995/96*. Hong Kong

2. Economic Intelligence Unit (1996). *Tourist Price Survey*. Hong Kong.

3. Hobson, Perry and Goldwyn Ko (1994). "Tourism and Politics: The Implications of the Change in Sovereignty on the Future Development of Hong Kong's Tourism Industry," *Journal of Travel Research* (Spring): pp. 2–8.

4. *Hong Kong Government Gazette, Special Supplement*, various issues. Hong Kong: Hong Kong Government Printer.

5. _____. *Annual Digest of Statistics*, various issues.

6. Hong Kong Hotels Association, Hong Kong Tourist Association, and Horwath Asia Pacific (1996). *Hong Kong Hotel Industry 1995/96*.

7. Hong Kong Tourist Association (1995). *A Statistical Review of Tourism 1994/95*, annual publication.

8. _____ (1995). *Visitor Profile Report* 1994/95, annual publication.

9. Hong Kong Tourist Association and Roger Tym & Partners (1995). *Visitor and Tourism Study for Hong Kong* (November).

10. Katz, Michael and Carl Shapiro (1985). "Network Externalities, Competition, and Compatibility," *American Economic Review Vol. 75*, No. 3: 424–440.

11. Kwong, Kai-Sun (1988). *Towards Open Skies and Uncongested Airport*. Hong Kong: Chinese University Press.

12. Lin, Tzong-Biau and Yun-Wing Sung (1983). "Hong Kong," in *Tourism in Asia: The Economic Impact*, eds., Elwood A. Pye and T.B. Lin, International Development Research Centre, Canada. Singapore: Singapore University Press.

13. Pacific Economic Cooperation Council (1996). *Pacific Economic Development Report 1995*. Singapore: Pacific Economic Cooperation Council.

14. Pacific Economic Cooperation Council and American Express Travel Related Company (1995). *Sourcebook on Travel and Tourism in the APEC Region*, (November). New York: American Express.

15. PKF Consulting Ltd (1996). *Trends in the Hotel Industry*, monthly publication. Hong Kong: PKF Consulting Ltd.

16. World Trade and Tourism Council (1996). *Singapore Travel and Tourism: Millenium Vision*, a WTTC Report (October). London: World Trade and Tourism Council.

Index

About the Author

Kai-Sun Kwong, PhD (British Columbia), is Associate Professor in the Department of Economics, The Chinese University of Hong Kong. He has served in a number of consultancy positions related to the industrial development in Hong Kong. In 1991 he served as consultant to the Industry Department of the Hong Kong Government on industrial pollution, in 1992 as consultant to the Technology Review Board of the Industry and Technology Development Council on technology assessment, and in 1994 as consultant to the World Bank on the mode of infrastructural development in Hong Kong. He has also been visiting scholar at the Department of Economics and the Stanford Institute of Theoretical Economics of Stanford University, California. He is the author of *Towards Open Skies and Uncongested Airports*, a publication of the Hong Kong Centre for Economic Research.

The Hong Kong Economic Policy Studies Series